ABOVE THE PACIFIC

ABOVE THE PACIFIC

Three Medal of Honor Fighter Aces of World War II Speak

COLIN HEATON

CALIBER

CALIBER

An imprint of Penguin Random House LLC
penguinrandomhouse.com

Copyright © 2023 by Colin D. Heaton
Penguin Random House supports copyright. Copyright fuels creativity,
encourages diverse voices, promotes free speech, and creates a vibrant culture.
Thank you for buying an authorized edition of this book and for complying with
copyright laws by not reproducing, scanning, or distributing any part of it in
any form without permission. You are supporting writers and allowing
Penguin Random House to continue to publish books for every reader.

DUTTON and the D colophon are registered trademarks
of Penguin Random House LLC.

LIBRARY OF CONGRESS CATALOGING-IN-PUBLICATION DATA
has been applied for.

ISBN 9780593471951 (paperback)
ISBN 9780593471968 (ebook)

Printed in the United States of America
1st Printing

For my dad, he was always my biggest fan

★ CONTENTS ★

ABOVE THE PACIFIC

★

COLONEL GREGORY BOYINGTON, USMC (RET.)

DECEMBER 4, 1912–JANUARY 11, 1988

Gregory Boyington is still revered today as a Marine Corps legend, fighter pilot, ace, and all-around "bad boy." But of all the interviews I've conducted over many years, Boyington was and remains the most controversial. Separating fact from fiction both during and after the interview process became an exercise in frustration: while much of the information Boyington gave me was challenged by others who were often present during certain events, other events were corroborated and even clarified.

General Curtis E. LeMay and General James H. Doolittle, mutual acquaintances, both warned me about Boyington's storytelling. But it was Doolittle who put me in touch with him. Doolittle's advice? "Just listen, record, and be prepared to be entertained." LeMay said, "Let me read that interview when you are done. I like reading good fiction." The late historian Jeffrey L. Ethell, my personal friend and mentor, also offered sage advice: "Boyington will spin any tall tale into a good story if you are willing to listen, but you have to buy the drinks."

I first called Boyington in 1982 after receiving a positive response to a letter I'd sent him. He was abrupt on the phone, but nevertheless agreed I could call again. Eventually, after we'd spoken several times, he told me that if I ever got to Fresno, he would give me an interview. He asked what I drank, and if I liked scotch. Unsure of where the conversation was going, I told him that I did enjoy a single malt on occasion. "Good, you are not a pussy, then," he said. What an introduction.

I arrived the morning of the interview ten minutes early. Boyington opened the door, said, "You're early," and shut the door. So I waited. At 0900 sharp the door opened again, and he greeted me as if he had never seen me before but was glad that I was there. As I walked in, he asked if I would like coffee. I said, "Yes, sir," and he asked how I liked it. I said black. "No, what do you like *in it?*" He pointed to several varieties of liquor, most of them scotch. I imbibed with him with a Johnnie Walker shot in my black coffee.

Boyington's house was neat, and his basement was a museum of artifacts, real treasures. His citations were framed nicely, and he happily personalized a print that I'd brought. He pointed to a stack of other prints and books, saying that he was yet to sign those, too. He freely spoke about his life, the war, and his personal issues, and he was never hesitant to call out people he thought were less than intelligent or dedicated. In that, he had a lot in common with LeMay, whom I interviewed two days later. (LeMay and I had a little discussion about my visit with Boyington, and LeMay said, "You look pretty good for a guy who had to walk through all that bullshit.")

Before the United States entered World War II, hundreds of Americans volunteered to serve in combat, many as pilots. Most expatriate fighter pilots flew for a paycheck, but many joined up just for the adventure. A good number who signed up to fight the Germans in 1940 with the Royal Air Force "Eagle Squadrons" did not return to American uniform until 1942, if at all. Others, like Boyington, served in the American Volunteer Group (AVG), the famed "Flying Tigers," a colorful group often labeled as "mercenaries," under Brigadier (later Major) General Claire Chennault in China and Burma.

Fighting in support of Chiang Kai-shek as the Japanese rampaged through China, the AVG was home to men who became legends, tough men doing a tough job in an inhospitable place where discipline was perhaps less important than getting results. Despite only being in combat from December 20, 1941, to July 4, 1942, they nevertheless became famed worldwide for their service, shooting down 229 Japanese aircraft and destroying another sixty-eight on the ground against a loss of just sixteen of their own forty members.

Gregory Boyington brought his skills and mindset to the war after several years as an instructor pilot with the United

States Marine Corps. He admitted that he was always eager to "mix it up" in a fight. Whether he was in the sky or in an officers' club, he admitted, his approach to life made him his "own worst enemy." Yet regardless of what people thought of Boyington as a person, all had to admit that he was the type of guy you wanted fighting your nation's enemies. His personal life was a combination of glory, exceptional (albeit controversial) service, and a lifelong struggle with alcoholism—the primary reason he had four wives and myriad severed professional and personal relationships. Speaking about Boyington, his fellow Medal of Honor recipient, Navy captain and top Navy fighter ace David McCampbell remarked: "If you have an event where alcohol is being served, protect your open bar. I would suggest armed security."

Colonel Gregory Boyington died of cancer on January 11, 1988, and was buried with full military honors at Arlington National Cemetery. A few years later, I was talking with World War II Marine Corps fighter pilot, Medal of Honor recipient, and South Dakota Air National Guard Brigadier General Joe Foss, and Boyington's name came up. "I wonder if they put a bottle of scotch in his casket," Foss said. "That would be the best send-off."

The following narrative is the result of a series of interviews I conducted with Greg Boyington by telephone from 1985 to 1986 and a personal interview conducted in 1986 at his home in Fresno, California.

GREGORY BOYINGTON

We were from Idaho originally, and I was born in Coeur d'Alene on December 4, 1912. The family moved to Oka-nogan, Washington, where my parents had an apple farm. As a kid I was into the outdoors, I liked that. My background is Sioux and Irish, so I guess I got the best and worst of both tribes in me. I hunted, fished, and read everything I could about the First World War pilots. I read the book by [Robert] Baden-Powell who started the Boy Scouts in England, and I saw myself as a kind of survivalist. I knew I was going to be a pilot. I felt that I was something of a tough guy.

When I was a teenager, I sort of had a reputation as a bully, or even an anti-bully. I never picked on other kids, but I was not a knight in shining armor going out of my way to help those being fucked with by bullies, either. But I did make a few exceptions. This one asshole was a guy about my size, named Harry-some-shit, and he would go around intimidating the other kids, shaking them down, just fucking with them. He beat up a few boys and took their money, one guy's watch. One guy he thumped was a buddy of mine.

Now, I had no problem letting two guys square off in a fair fight, but this guy Harry was not like that. He was an ambush predator, a real prick. He did not want to fight; he just wanted to ambush kids and steal shit. I was not down with that at all, I can tell you. That dickhead was on my shit list. One day in school I called him out, and he seemed to enjoy the prospect of the fight. "After school, be there," I told him, and he agreed. Well, after school, I went to the arranged location, populated by just about every kid in school waiting to see this great struggle, and he was nowhere to be seen.

I waited for almost an hour and had started to walk home when I heard something in the woods to my left. It was Harry, the asshole. He was waiting to ambush me away from prying eyes, hoping to get the drop on me. He fucked up. I had been learning boxing, and I was pretty good at it. He ran at me full speed and raised his right arm to lay down a haymaker. I saw that shit coming from downtown, and I just blocked his swing with my left arm and leaned into a full-throat punch with my right, using all my weight.

He went down like a bag of bricks. I punched him a few more times, just to make sure that he bore the marks of an ass beating in school. That would let everyone know that he was not invincible. I broke his nose, and my knuckles were bloody from his teeth, and I know that he lost at least one. I then told him that if he ever tried to do another shakedown, I would find him and kill him, no shit, certain death, not an ass beating. I was tired of that shit. I do not believe he ever fucked with another student again.

Well, my parents heard about it, and I was called into the principal's office. Harry was there with his dad, and he was looking pretty bad. His head was swollen, his jaw looked like it was stuffed, and he had raccoon eyes where his nose was broken. He was all black-and-blue. I did not have a mark on me except my knuckles, and I almost felt sorry for him. It came down to my word against his as to how that ass beating went down, but the principal had heard from other kids that he had attacked them. I told my story, which was supported by a few kids who knew we were supposed to meet. I was given a warning about fighting in school and told I would be expelled if it happened again. Harry got the same lecture, and I felt that the entire situation had been handled fairly. Since it happened off school grounds, there was not too much the principal could even do about it.

The one thing about America back then was the crazy interest in anything related to aviation. Barnstormers crossed the country like carrier pigeons. I saw some air shows, took a few rides, and I was hooked hard on flying. I was impressed by the barnstorming pilots, especially guys like Clyde Pangborn. I guess I was about six or seven years old, and I got a ride. That was probably the best day of my life. I was so impressed, I knew what I was going to do when I grew up. There was no way in hell I was not going to become a pilot. While in high school I wrestled, played football, and was just really into sports. I was very competitive, to the point of being dangerous.

I liked girls, too, but I never got into trouble there. My grades were pretty good. I did well in math and English, but I liked history a lot, so I did not really have to be prodded to study. I sort of absorbed information; it stuck with me. I built all the airplane models, read all the books I could about flying and pilots, especially the First World War pilots from all the countries—my mind was set. After I survived high school, I attended the University of Washington. I saw that as an avenue into aviation training and I earned a bachelor's degree in aeronautical engineering. This was a really new degree program because aviation was still new.

I thought pretty hard about my options, looking at bomber and fighter pilots. Billy Mitchell had made history, so he was an idol, just like Charles Lindbergh when he crossed the Atlantic. Eddie Rickenbacker, Frank Luke, the Red Baron [Manfred von Richthofen], Mick Mannock, Albert Ball—all these guys were fighter pilots. They were my heroes as pilots. That was what I wanted to be. It was more than a desire. I felt it was my destiny.

In college I had to work to make extra money, so I was a parking attendant and did other shit. I had a loan shark ask me to work as a collection agent. I did that for a short time, but I realized that if I was caught roughing clowns up to collect money that I would have a record and that would kill flying. I was in the Army ROTC program at that time anyway and had started flight training. I became an aviation cadet in 1934 and completed ground and basic flight training in 1935.

I did well, passed all the prerequisites the first time, high marks, and then went on to advanced training and earned my wings in 1937. Before all that, I had met a recruiting officer from the Navy recruiting graduates for that service. I told him I was interested and I wanted to fly. He did not seem too supportive of my desire, telling me that naval aviation was hard to get into, that the [naval] academy grads got first choice on those billets. I thought that was total bullshit.

I also had a similar talk with an Army officer. He told me the same thing about the West Point guys getting first shot at the flying schools and said that my chances were limited. Again bullshit, I thought. Luckily, I was able to get my training through the school, which had a deal with the military for officers' training. But I sort of had another problem. I had gotten married to Helen in college, and they were not taking married men into the flight programs. Actually, that was a major problem, so I adopted the last name "Boyington" to get by. My real dad and my mom split when I was a crawler, and I'd gone by "Hallenbeck" growing up. "Boyington" was my natural [biological] father's last name, but since I would have no record of marriage as "Boyington," that worked for me.

In 1934 I had been assigned as a second lieutenant in the Army Coastal Reserve [630th Coastal Artillery battery] in Washington, and that bullshit was just not for me. It was boring as hell and not doing me any damned good. I had an opportunity to speak with a Marine Corps pilot, the first one I ever met. I don't remember his rank, but he was a really squared-away fellow. He helped me get through the paperwork, gave me some advice, and I joined the Corps as an already qualified pilot. That was a real bonus, having a pilot's license, I can tell you, and also being instrument rated.

In 1936 I went to Pensacola, where I sailed through basic and advanced flight schools, and I graduated the next year as a Marine Corps pilot. I went to Quantico in 1937, and then to Philadelphia for a year, and finished in 1939. I went through the required training courses, even infantry training. That was the way the Marines worked; every Marine was a rifleman first. What you did after that was a MOS [Military Occupational Specialty]. The Corps then sent me to San Diego, where I carrier-qualified flying off the *Yorktown* and *Lexington*.

Taking off and landing on a carrier is a head rush, no shit about it. I got good at trapping. You have to remember that back then, there were no totally reliable catapults to launch aircraft from a carrier deck. You still had to turn the ship into the wind, and then use full throttle for a full-power takeoff to get speed and distance once you left the deck. You pulled back on the stick to get lift once your airspeed was adequate to avoid a stall and then trimmed your plane.

After all that was completed, I had orders back to Pensacola in 1940. They made me a basic flight and instrumentation instructor. Not bad duty, standard working hours with plenty of time to hit the "O" [officers'] club. I was then assigned all over hell and high water, but getting some good flight time in. At least they made me a basic flight instructor, which was better than sitting behind a desk somewhere. That would have been a death sentence.

While in Florida, I was able to fly in a few competitions, such as the Miami Air Races. Jimmy Doolittle was also a major participant in a lot of these events for many years. That was when

I first met him, at an air race. Doolittle is a hell of a nice guy, I have to say.

Hell, I would have flown a case of beer just to log more air time, because that was where your experience came in. It also helped to have a lot of air time when going for promotions.

I continued flying and instructing, but I also read all of the newspapers I could get my hands on. I was up to speed on what the hell was going on in Asia and Europe. I knew that eventually we were going to get involved, and I was not going to miss out on the action. Kind of like walking into a casino with a pocket full of coins—you know that sure as shit you're going to hit those slot machines.

The Japs were overrunning China, and I knew soon it would be the entire Asian continent. I saw the Chinese government was hiring people, especially pilots. I made a long-distance call to a number I'd been given by a guy I knew in flight school and spoke to a fellow, a nice enough guy, about the particulars of the job. He said that former military pilots were being selected for a special unit to work in China. He emphasized "former." I was also informed that it would be illegal for a serving commissioned officer to go fly for a foreign country, so I resigned my commission. The pay was far better and with bonuses for fighter pilots who scored kills. I needed the money, so I signed up in September of 1941.

The [1st] American Volunteer Group [originally known as the Central Aircraft Manufacturing Company (CAMCO)] was paying $675 per month plus a bonus of $500 for every confirmed scalp you knocked down. In 1941, that was the same as making $5,000 a month today [1986], and with me having an ex-wife, three kids, debts, and my lifestyle, I really needed the work. Hell, just the standard salary was almost ten times my Marine Corps pay. Besides, the government knew damned well what we were doing. They set it all up, [President Franklin D.] Roosevelt and that crew.

That was when I learned that [Admiral Chester W.] Nimitz maintained files of all Navy and Marine pilots and ground crews going over. I can only assume he knew we were going to be in the war as well, and wanted to have an immediate source file to recall combat pilots. That made perfect sense to me. Why would the government not want a ready reservoir of trained pilots when the shit hit the fan? The only catch was that we had to be secret about the whole affair.

Those of us who were accepted for work all went to San Francisco, where we boarded a Dutch ship called the *Boschfontein*, an old tramp steamer of some kind. Everybody had a cover story. My personal cover was that I was going to Java to fly for KLM Airlines. Some of the guys got really seasick, but I was pretty much OK. I had brought a good bottle of scotch along. Well, a few bottles actually. I wasn't sure what the scotch supply would be like when we arrived. I had no idea if even the water was drinkable. Need to be prepared, you know?

The first time I met Claire Chennault was in a village called Toungoo, right outside Rangoon, Burma. This place was a real shithole, I tell you. A real one-water-buffalo town. Every little village had a chief, and this one was no exception, although the British were pretty much running the show there. To be fair, most of these local people were very friendly. They knew what the Japs were doing, and that we were there to help, so they treated us well.

Chennault was very impressive in appearance and commanded respect, although some of his decisions later alienated him from many of us. Frankly, he just pissed me off. He had issues with us and some of our antics, such as shooting down telephone lines with our Colt forty-fives on the train to our billets, holding water buffalo races and rodeos in the street, or shooting up the chandeliers in a bar when they quit serving us. Some of the ground crew had been caught smuggling guns and liquor for profit, and that went over like a mortar round.

One of our last stunts was to fly the Chiangs on an escort mission. Before this, we were told to give an air show, a flyby for the benefit of the Chiangs, Chennault, and some other dignitaries. Those of us in the flight had a plan. We passed by so low in a rolling turn that they all fell flat on the deck. I guess this was the last straw for Chennault.

My opinion of Chennault began to go downhill fast following his orders for a greater effort in ground-attack missions. These missions were costing us in aircraft and pilots for no appreciable gain. The 3rd Squadron [Hell's Angels] was unusually busy, attacking imaginary depots and "unknown numbers of troops in the field."

It was all complete bullshit for the most part, and he had to have known it. Sometimes we had legitimate targets that we could confirm, and those were OK, but you still ran the risk of small arms nailing you. We were not even able to do a post-battle damage assessment most of the time, as we did not have a photo-recon plane to shoot post-operation pictures. It was all for local public consumption, to justify getting more money spent and for Chennault to get good press. Chennault just wanted to keep the reports active once we ran out of Japanese planes to tangle with.

Many of the pilots refused to fly these missions, since there was no bonus for killing a tree. When Chennault threatened some of us with courts-martial, that really began the tide rolling against him. We reminded him that we were civilian specialists—contractors, I guess you could say—working for a foreign government, not his personal command. He had no legal authority to invoke anything resembling military prosecution. He was screwed on that and he knew it; the bluff backfired. Finally, Chennault negotiated extra money for strafing, and I volunteered. So did a few others, including [Dick] Rossi, [Charles "Chuck"] Older, [David Lee "Tex"] Hill, and [John] Newkirk.

Chennault may have been a real prima donna prick, but the greatest thorn in my side was the executive officer, Harvey Greenlaw, although his wife was hot. This clown was not a friendly type, and he prepared the paperwork for a court-martial on me, Lewis Bishop, and John Croft for "conduct unbecoming officers," all because we had been holding rickshaw races with the locals. I think he was of the opinion that I had been too friendly with his wife, Olga, and not just me. I will let that lie as it is. Well, among the many issues he had with us, he saw us pulling these two rickshaws with the drivers sitting in luxury as our passengers. The bitch of it was that we had to pay those drivers for the privilege of pulling their fucking rickshaws.

I told that bastard Greenlaw that if he continued being a thorn in my side, I would introduce him to some old-fashioned hooking and jabbing. I also told him that accidents happened, and sometimes those Jap bombs that laid around unexploded had the habit of going off unexpectedly and you never knew who might get hit. If there was ever anybody whose coffee I would have liked to piss in, it was that asshole's. He finally got the message much later. The thought of rolling a grenade into his tent crossed my mind, I can tell you. What a prick.

Our living conditions were absolutely the worst shitholes you could imagine. People did their toilet business right in the street. Sanitation was unheard of, and the various diseases that we witnessed were enough to convert even the most adventurous of Romeos to celibacy. There were these dogs, real nasty mongrels that were wild and fed off the dead and dying people. The smells were indescribable. The greatest problem was the rat infestation. We made traps and all sorts of shit to try and get rid of them. One of the guys said he would get some poison for them, and soon he managed to get some strychnine or cyanide, something like that. He baited some food with the poison at various places.

The outhouse was a great target of opportunity. Guys coming out at night often stepped on one. One of the ground crew was bitten in his rack. We had a generator to operate a few lights; otherwise we had oil lamps and candles. One night the lights were cut on briefly for a P-40 to land, and we had a few cars with their headlights on alongside the runway. The entire landing strip seemed to be moving. It was a rat migration or something. Incredible sight, really. We could not get rid of the damned things. We hired some local boys to hunt them down, which they did. They ate the damned things. I was offered some roasted rat, but passed on that. I would stick to water buffalo steaks or canned meat.

There were so many stories about these locals that they could fill a book. There was this one guy, and he had a pet cobra. I see your face [referring to Heaton]—yes, a cobra. He kept that bastard in a canvas bag, and he would pull it out and show people for a fee. I saw it and it had to be at least eight feet long. I asked one of the interpreters if the guy had ever been bitten. "No," I was told, the toothless old fool had never been bitten. Later on, I heard that it did bite him, and he died. I guess it takes all kinds.

Another reason Chennault was pissed at a few of us in general, and me in particular, was we would have rifles out and go hunting. I think it was Charlie Bond who came up with the idea. There were wild pigs running around, but we also had a monkey problem. These damned monkeys were destructive, thieving bastards. Once we heard a ground crewman yelling, and some of us stepped out. He was jumping up and down—this damned monkey had left a tent and was hauling ass down the dirt side road, dragging a cartridge belt and holster with a forty-five in it. When some of the guys got close to it, it slipped the forty-five out of the holster.

We were not too worried about it because you had to cock the pistol before it would fire, but you still did not want to lose a weapon, as we all had to sign for them. Well, this guy went to get the pistol from the monkey, and the monkey was not having any of it. It was really aggressive. When the mechanic came closer, the monkey dropped the gun and jumped on his ass, scratching and biting him. He was bloody as hell, and he beat that damned monkey damned near to death. Another guy pulled his sidearm and shot the monkey.

Now we had a real problem. We had been warned about rabies in the local animals. We had no medical facilities, so we had to take the monkey and the mechanic into Rangoon, and then to India. From what I heard, the monkey was not rabid, but the mechanic had to have surgery to reattach his left thumb and stitches in his face and on his arms. Well, after that, some of us went monkey hunting. We were shooting those suckers out of the trees. Our hope was that they would be too scared to come back. They weren't completely stupid. Hell, they were smarter than some officers I knew. Chennault heard about that shit and called us on the carpet. We defended our actions by saying it was pest control to protect the men, and he let that ride.

We always had these tiger scares. The locals lived in fear of them, and you heard these stories about them killing someone.

We did not have a tiger kill anyone while we were there, but one night one of our perimeter sentries heard what he thought was a tiger. He alerted the rest of the guards and they spread the word to be extra cautious. Ben Foshee and I decided to make a tiger trap. The next day we hired some locals and had them dig a deep-ass pit about fifteen feet deep and ten feet square. Then we had some bamboo stakes sharpened and cut to about three feet long. We buried them vertically to impale the tiger if it fell in. I wanted a tiger skin to take home; that would have been great.

Then we covered it with light bamboo rods and grass to camouflage it. We baited the center with a dead chicken, sure that it would draw the tiger to an easy meal. Well, two nights later, we heard a big squeal and crash, and knew we got something. We decided to wait until sunrise when we could see what the hell it was. When we went to the trap, we saw that we had caught a large boar. It was still alive, so I fired a round into it. Well, we were disappointed that it was not the tiger, but we barbecued that big bastard and had a feast.

Then, if this shit was not already crazy as hell, one of our guys living in one of the tents near the end of the strip failed to report the next morning. Tex [Hill] sent one of the guys to go check on him, and he came back running, out of breath and white as a snowstorm. He was yelling "big fucking snake" over and over again, so we got to the tent. Sure as horseshit, the guy was in his hammock and a large-ass python had coiled its body around him. His head was cocked over at us, and his eyes were the size of hubcaps. He was scared shitless and I could not blame him.

Well, we had to get that big-ass snake off of him, so I told someone to find where the head was. One guy located it, and another pilot—I think it was Rossi, not sure—grabbed its tail. Anyway, we wrestled that big bitch off the poor guy. It took five of us, and when we killed it, the thing measured twenty-five feet long and weighed at least two hundred pounds, if not more. We gave it to the villagers, and they were happier than pimps on payday. They ate them, you know. Hell, I think they ate everything with a pulse, to be honest.

[The AVG had] three flights. The 1st Squadron was "Adam and Eve," which I was assigned to. The 2nd Squadron was the "Panda Bears" commanded by Jack Newkirk, while the 3rd Squadron was the "Hell's Angels" led by [Arvid] Olson. My squadron saw the least combat and was the last to really get involved in the action. Each squadron had twenty pilots and was completely staffed with ground crews, including mechanics, avionics, and weapons specialists. [*Historian Barrett Tillman disputes these numbers since the AVG had about a hundred pilots and sixty Navy/Marine Corps. (Note to author, March 20, 2021)*] Those were good guys, dedicated and very solid, I can say for the most part. We rarely had enough operational aircraft for all the pilots. Maintenance suffered because we had a hard time getting spare parts, and the Warhawks were all so worn out that I worried about some of them even being airworthy. [*Tillman believes that instead of being worn out, the AVG planes might have been diverted directly from a UK shipment. He does not recall any other Tigers making similar comments. (Note to author, March 20, 2021) In interviews I conducted, Chuck Older, Tex Hill, and Dick Rossi also contradicted Boyington's statement.*]

I began flying familiarization with the Curtis P-40s we had been issued, as well as the P-36 types that were around. This was in November 1941. The P-40s were aircraft that we had lend-leased to Britain and were loaned from the RAF [Royal Air Force] to us again. We got the idea to paint shark mouths on them after someone found a picture in a magazine showing a RAF P-40 in North Africa painted that same way, so we kind of stole the idea.

My first flight in a P-40 was something of a show, since I had always preferred to make three-point contact landings in the planes back in Florida. I had the cockpit check and took off, and when I tried to land, I bounced, so I slammed the throttle forward for another go-around. The result was a ruptured manifold gauge, and when I landed, I was given a stern reprimand about gunning the Allison engines. My argument was that these secondhand fighters were so worn out, it would not take much for them to break down. I started flying combat with "Adam and Eve" [1st] squadron in early December, and I remember thinking when we heard about Pearl Harbor that it was only a matter of time before we were brought back into the U.S. military. That would mean less money.

Rumors abounded that we were going to be disbanded and all pilots and ground crews would be drafted back into the military into each man's respective branch of service. Then there was the rumor that [General] Hap Arnold was going to place us all in the Army to fly. Those of us who were not Army were not too happy to hear that kind of shit, and besides, the AVG gig was better money. We were still doing the same job, just better paychecks. Right after we arrived in Rangoon, we took off on a "bogey" [unidentified aircraft] call on January 26, 1942, and ran into around fifty to sixty Japs. We were severely outnumbered by the enemy, who were flying I-97 [Nakajima Ki-27]-type fighters. They were about two thousand feet above us and diving down. Pretty soon I was all alone, as everybody else decided to run for the deck. I pulled over to the right to avoid the crowd, and I spotted two I-97s and closed with them. As I fired at one, the other pulled a loop over me, so I had to break off and compensate for the maneuver. I just gave up and followed suit, heading for the deck like the rest of the guys.

Then I suddenly pulled up and climbed. I spotted another [enemy] fighter and decided to drop the nose and close in, firing as I gained on him. Suddenly, as he was almost filling the windscreen, he performed a split S that any instructor would have envied, and I then noticed that I was not alone. His friends had joined in. I got smart real fast, again took another dive, and ran for home, no claims. When I landed, I found a Jap 7.7-millimeter bullet in my arm, an incendiary that gave me a nice scar. I also found that I had been reported as shot down. I think Dick Rossi was also listed as shot down, because he arrived later after dodging a few. I think he also got a kill, but he claimed a damaged that was later confirmed, if memory serves. [*Rossi did get the credit.*]

That first crack at the Japs was a disaster, and all of us were seriously upset with our dismal performance, especially since my rickshaw-racing buddy, [Louis] "Cokey" Hoffman, had been killed. Losing him was a real morale dump because he was the most experienced pilot, an old-school type and a great guy. He was prior Army and Navy and had flown just about everything we had. The first kill for me came three days after this. I got two, and the flight scored a total of sixteen with no losses to us. Rossi had scored. The next kills came soon after. We had already taken off on two false ground alarms. Probably another damned tiger was spotted, for all I knew. Finally, on the third hop, I saw a lone I-97 and took him out over the bay at the Settang River.

I got three more on one mission, two of them close together. The third was an open-cockpit fighter, and took a long time to go down, even after I popped a lot of shells into it. I increased power and pulled up next door and looked over. I saw the pilot was dead, but the plane kept on flying. I slipped behind him and fired one well-placed burst to finish him off and collect the money. At that point I had six confirmed victories with the AVG. [*Actual AVG records credit Boyington with 3.5 victories.*]

We were lied to about everything [related to flying conditions]. The aircraft were garbage, with spare parts being a virtual unknown, and all with tired engines barely able to get us off the ground. The Brits had run these damned things into the ground, so that explained why they were more than happy to pass them off to us. Some of them had been patched so many times from bullet holes that I'm certain they would not have passed an airframe certification back in the States.

The maps we were supposed to use were the worst I'd ever seen. Whoever made those maps had either never been to those places, was more drunk than I was, or was having a bad acid trip when they sat down to create those worthless objects. Some points of reference were more than a hundred miles off, and the magnetic declination was worthless. The weather could also get you into trouble, and we had no meteorological reports, not like today, and not even as good as what we had later during the Pacific campaign. We flew near the mountains and that weather changed every hour. No two days were the same.

At Kunming we had a seven-thousand-foot-long runway that never seemed to get completed, even after five years of constant work, until our military came in well into the war. I always wondered if the assholes building that thing were getting paid by the foot. Now, take into account the greatest lie of all: that the Japanese pilots were pathetic and lacked good vision. I can tell you from firsthand experience that some of the best men to ever fly a plane in combat were the Japanese, especially the Imperial Navy pilots. Well, perhaps except for us. Those guys were no fucking joke. If you screwed up, you were done for. We also never had radar or anything resembling a modern air-warning system.

However, we did have a series of visual lookouts and a system of telephone relays, and considering the hundreds of dialects and different languages on this massive line system, things still got done. Sometimes the telephone system was out of whack due to weather, or maybe a monkey pulling down a wire. One time we had a series of visual relays. The warning that shit was coming was when a yahoo began waving a rice-threshing rake and screaming something. This happened once and we all began heading for the planes. Then one of the guys who spoke English said that it was not incoming enemy aircraft. The guy had seen a tiger. Go figure.

The [Mitsubishi A6M] Zero was legendary in its agility, due to its light weight and turning radius. The power-to-weight ratio was incredible. No one could turn inside a Zero. I spoke to a Brit Hurricane pilot who fought them, and he said that the Zero was the only plane that could turn inside a Hurricane, but that both were evenly matched overall, except that the Mark II Hurricane had better armament with cannons. A Zero could not catch us in a dive while flying a P-40, but they could sure as happy shit outclimb us, almost a two-to-one climb ratio. However, most of our fights were against other aircraft, like the I-97. We developed the tactics of a hit-and-run dive down from higher altitude and strike, continue the dive, and convert airspeed into altitude for another attack. [*Boyington misidentified the aircraft. There were no Zeros in China or Burma at that time. The aircraft flown by the Japanese were the Ki-43 Oscars. (Tillman, note to author, March 25, 2021)*]

The other plus for us was that we flew three-element flights, with the top cover waiting until the other two had attacked. Once the Japs scrambled to intercept us, the top cover would swoop down and pick them off. We also had the advantage of heavier armament, two or four fifty-caliber and sometimes four thirty-caliber machine guns, with later versions having all fifties, against their two 7.7-millimeter guns, and later versions had the twenty-millimeter cannon. Not every P-40 was uniform in its armament, due to resources, the variant, or some required field-modified configurations.

A lot of it depended on what guns were available, as we did not get a regular resupply. We went through barrels, which had to be replaced, and a lot of the time the ammo was worthless, probably due to the high humidity or just old bullets. Hell, that ammo and other supplies probably passed through more hands than a five-dollar bill at a poker party. We also had the great advantage of armor plate in the cockpit and self-sealing fuel tanks. The Japs had none of them, sacrificing pilot safety for range, speed, and maneuverability, and it cost them dearly throughout the war. Just a couple of well-placed incendiaries could torch a Jap plane, or hard-ball rounds through the cockpit would kill the pilot.

You could best compare it to fencing with a foil against a broadsword. Another great advantage was communications. We all had radios when they worked, but very few Jap fighters carried them—to reduce weight and extend their range, from what I understand. I found that crazy. Good communication is part of great teamwork. I could not imagine going into combat without a radio. That would be like screwing a well-used local hooker without a condom. It was just not the right thing to do.

On December 30 [1941], the 2nd Squadron ["Panda Bears"] moved south from Toungoo to Mingaladon with a lot of new aircraft [eighteen new P-40s], relieving the 3rd Squadron ["Hell's Angels"], who had been there since December 12. They all shared the air defense of Rangoon with two British units. [*No. 17 Squadron using Hawker Hurricanes and No. 67 Squadron with Brewster Buffaloes.*]

Another event occurred on February 7, 1942, when [Robert] "Sandy" Sandell, the group leader, was killed test-flying his P-40. RAF witnesses said he inverted and appeared to be stalling, but that he recovered. It would appear that he pulled back on the stick too hard and half rolled into an inverted crash. That was a sad day; he was a great guy. And he was a great pilot, so I am certain that it was not pilot error. As I said before, these P-40s were shit. I think Tex [Hill] once took off and a piston cracked and he had to abort. I know that Newkirk once had a similar incident when he took off and oil sprayed his windscreen. Apparently, the oil line blew or something.

We had a lot of accidents, but nothing too terrible. Our greatest enemies were weather and bad maintenance, not the Japs. We were able to handle them without much problem. We used better tactics, our P-40s were armored, and we had confidence. I do not want to disparage all the mechanics. Some were great, some were shit, but all had to work with what they had. Cannibalizing a fighter became standard to keep others flying, until we had new birds. Sometimes the Japs got really lucky.

That is not to say that the Japs were idiots. Many of these guys had been flying combat for almost a decade, and they knew their business. Despite flying outdated "Vic" formations [three-aircraft "V" formations] and not having better armor and self-sealing tanks, those fuckers could outmaneuver anything in the sky. That was the first rule we were told upon arrival: "Do not try and turn with a Zero when you encounter it. You will not like the results." That was why we developed the hit-and-run attack method with one flight as top cover and another below as either bait or to catch the enemy in a dive trying to escape. The second flight would be the primary, so we could sort of box them into the kill zone, so to speak. It usually worked out well.

Once, we had an air raid over the strip, and I jumped into my P-40. To make a long story short, the maintenance had not been carried out and I crashed, really banging myself up. Just after takeoff, I lost power and crashed into a rice paddy. My seat belt broke and my head slammed into the gunsight, and I slammed my knees into the instrument panel, cracking the kneecaps, but I managed to crawl out of the wreckage, which did not take too goddamned long, I can tell you, as I was afraid of fire. Busted knees or not, I thought that I could have given Jesse Owens a run for his money. I was barely able to make it. I made it my mission in life to find that crew chief later, but that is a story better left untold. You know, statute of limitations and shit. [*According to witnesses at the time, Boyington was drunk when he tried to take off. Crew Chief Leo Schramm said, "Boyington got out and ran straight to a water truck, started it up, and drove away, not returning for hours." The truck was later found where a tree had stopped it. "Apparently, he was not satisfied with just destroying an airplane."*]

To make matters worse, we had a wedding one evening shortly after that. One of our guys from 3rd Squadron, Fred Hodges, got married. During the ceremony the air-raid horn sounded, and I decided to hobble out wearing a bathrobe and jump into a trench. I actually jumped off a cliff in the dark, further injuring myself and undoing the repair work that had been performed on me previously. After that, I was flown to Kunming and placed in a hospital. Within a few weeks, I had my knees taped up really good and began flying again.

Many strange things happened. Once, two [RAF Hawker] Hurricane pilots had been flying above fifty Japs of the main force. They saw a P-40 and they thought he would join them, but instead the AVG pilot threw himself into the whole [enemy] group, with Japs all around him, guns blazing and confusion all over the place. The two Brits dropped to assist, cursing the crazy man who had started the melee. They all managed to get out of it. When I talked to one of the Brits, he dropped a 7.7-millimeter slug onto the bar. He had found it in his parachute after he landed. The American pilot in the P-40 turned out to be Jim Howard. It figured he would get the Medal of Honor for doing the same thing against the Germans later.

One thing I would like to mention is those British and Australian pilots. We crossed with them sometimes, and I will say that they were sharp guys, if a little stiff, you know. This one Hurricane pilot was flying north of Rangoon and we had a patrol. We could sometimes tune in to the same radio channel to simplify shit, and this time there was a battle. He and his flight were jumped. They called out on open frequency and they put up a good fight. We were too far away to be involved—in fact, we did not even know where they were, exactly.

Later, one of the Australian or British pilots I'd met before told Ed Rector and me what had happened. They had a fight with Zeros and this young guy was hit and he caught fire. The Hurricane was fabric covered, and his canopy was jammed. He radioed that he could not bail out. He tried to find a place to land that thing, and he finally did, sliding across a rice paddy. But he could not get out, and his friends flew over, circling, hoping a villager would come to his aid. All they could do was circle, watching helplessly as this guy just burned to death, black smoke pouring up into the sky.

The pilot said that they could hear his screams over the radio as he sat in that funeral pyre, breaking the glass to try and get out, until the radio went silent. It never exploded; it just burned, like a fucking Viking funeral. The boy I spoke with must have been about twenty, a two-year combat veteran, and he cried like a baby as he told me. I am not an emotional guy, never have been, unless it was anger, but I cried with him. I knew the kid who died. He was about nineteen years old, I think. He had been a pilot for about a year. His rank was flight sergeant, if I recall correctly. He was going home in a couple of weeks after getting permission to get married. I really felt like shit after hearing that story. Suddenly, my world did not seem so bad. Rector said, "Could be any one of us at any time; you just never know."

They did not come any better [than General "Vinegar Joe" Stilwell]. He was a real fighter. The British really harangued Stilwell because Burma fell and continued to be occupied. Hell, they lost the damned thing, not us. They always failed to mention that he had only Burmese, Indian, and Chinese troops under his command—no British or American forces until later, and they were not adequately supplied. They hardly had any radios. The language barriers alone would kill effective operations. Until they began getting major airdrops, most of the weapons they used were taken from dead Japs. They had no proper antimalarial drugs, no chloroquine, so dysentery plagued the men. Many were ill and had no food. They were just living off the land or whatever friendly villagers gave them to eat.

Despite all of that, he fought a good delaying operation. Stilwell was a real soldier, even if he was a West Pointer, and he thought no more of sharing a can of grub with an enlisted man than pulling his boots on. But he was also accused of being indifferent to their suffering. He led by extraordinary example, which was probably one of the many reasons the established Sandhurst and Oxbridge crowd [Oxford and Cambridge graduates] disliked him. He was good at his job and had tallied up a great body count of Japs, despite not having a proper force. Few people have earned my respect, but he's one of them. Mostly, I guess, because he kept Chiang in check, and he really pissed off the British and Chennault. He was not out to make friends, and he let everyone know it. He turned pissing people off into an art form. My kind of guy.

The AVG was being disbanded by July 4, 1942, and Chennault informed us that we all were to be inducted as lieutenants in the Army Air Corps, regardless of past affiliation. I did not agree with that arrangement, especially since I was the only regular pilot in my squadron and the rest were reservists. [*Boyington was granted a regular commission on the grounds that "he not return" as chronicled by Bruce Gamble in* Black Sheep One: The Life of Gregory "Pappy" Boyington.] I had a major's commission waiting in Washington with the Marine Corps, and I was not about to sacrifice my gold wings for dead lead. Besides, I was still pissed off about my back pay, and the fact that I had three kills yet to be confirmed because of "lost after-action reports." My ass. I needed that money.

I mentioned a written agreement that I had with Nimitz, but Chennault was having none of it. He said that he would personally see that my ass stayed right under his command once we transitioned back into the U.S. military. That way he could court-martial me and do it legally. Screw that. Besides, majors make more than lieutenants, and when I heard about this from Chennault, my Sioux-Irish blood began to boil. I was not alone, either. Besides, Chennault had pissed me off when he placed a two-drink maximum on my nights out. He told my own pilots to spy on me, and they told me about it. Rossi even came to me and said, "We have our differences, Greg, but I am not real comfortable with the general's tactics." Rector told me, "He's just waiting for you to screw up and be caught drunk. He wants your ass, so be forewarned."

Then I get a note that I was being charged $200 for killing a water buffalo. Greenlaw said they would take it out of my pay. I went fucking berserk and asked him what the hell he was talking about. He said that a farmer filed a claim that I had killed his water buffalo by shooting it in a rice paddy as target practice. I asked him when this was supposed to have happened. He told me the date, location, and time. I asked if he had any proof that the buffalo had been killed, and he said they did not have any direct evidence, just a bloodstain on the ground.

I asked Greenlaw how in the hell did he know it wasn't killed for steaks, and they just wanted a payday? How did they identify the plane or pilot? He said he "had sources" and I told him he "had shit." I also told him that either he was lying, the prick rice farmer was lying, or Chennault put him up to it. That shit could bring a criminal charge against me, and they would push it to make a point for PR purposes. Greenlaw smiled his shit-eating grin. "We have you now, Boyington," he said, smiling.

I stood up, looked him in the eye, and told him, "You don't have shit, you asshole, and I can file charges against your ass for making a false statement, because you were too fucking stupid or lazy to investigate. If your head was not up your ass, you would have checked the unit diary. I was in fucking India, asshole. I did not get back until three weeks after this supposed shit happened." The color drained from his face. It really was priceless. "Now, pay me my goddamned money." What he did not know, and I did know, was that most of the entire AVG were within earshot of that conversation. It was over for Greenlaw, and his backwards ass knew it. He had just lost all credibility. Rossi told me afterward, "You could have been more diplomatic."

He [Greenlaw] was Chennault's hatchet man and was like Chennault, a real bastard. That prick even had spies watching me. He was also less than pleased by the fact that we all enjoyed the company of the local girls on occasion, and I was no angel. I admit it. Another thing that irritated many of us was when the incompetent administration staff told us that we could not get paid for our kills, or even for our monthly back pay, because they had lost some of the after-action reports. That was the responsibility of Greenlaw. I wanted to pay that bastard a visit, but Tex told me not to. Then Chennault issued an order for us to fly certain missions again. I told everyone that my ass was not even taking off until they paid me. We were contractors, not his damned serfs.

Well, a few of us were talking, and none of us were happy about it. I hauled my ass across the air base and stormed in to see Greenlaw. He was not there, but Olga was and she said that was up to someone else handling payroll, and without the reports there could be no bonus verification. I was asking her about our base pay. At least we could get that? Again, she said that had to come through Chennault, and that made me even more furious. I told her that I knew damned well that they were not lost, and everyone knew what had happened. They were going to steal our pay for themselves, those bastards.

Tex Hill and [John] Newkirk kept copies of those reports and handed them in for their guys, and I made a statement that I knew Chennault and his staff clowns got their fucking pay. I accused Chennault, Greenlaw, and company of stealing our money, and Greenlaw said he would court-martial me. I made some smart-ass comment that since we were not in the actual United

States military as of that moment, the best he could do was to send me the bill for his dental reconstruction.

He said he would have me on charges for threatening a superior officer. I told him that if he could find an officer who was superior to me outside of rank, then I would like to meet him. He really pissed me off then. There was no way in hell I was staying under that asshole's command. I told a couple of the guys that we should wait for Chennault to land his personal aircraft, then at night paint red meatballs on it. That way we could shoot it down and have plausible deniability. Rossi said I was nuts for even thinking that. Another guy said he could get the paint. To hell with this, I was going, and there was nothing Chennault could do about it, even if I had to steal a plane to get the hell out of there.

I was also a little less than pleased with Chiang Kai-shek. Chiang was a legalized bandit, a crook big-time, and everyone knew it. He pretended to command the Chinese Army fighting the Japs, while he was still fighting the communists in the north as they fought the Japs. He just could not make up his damned mind. He got real rich off the war, and I know he was profiteering from all the Allied aid coming in. He kept bitching about needing more aid before he could commit troops to help Stilwell, but Stilwell apparently had the ledgers showing that Chiang was getting better and more numerous supply shipments than he was, and he was the damned commander.

Chiang lived a pretty lavish lifestyle. We pilots were his personal guests once, and his world was a completely different planet from the way his people lived. I knew that Chiang was stockpiling his weapons and ammunition, holding out for more shit so that he would be in a better position to wipe out Mao [Zedong] and the communists once the Japs were gone. It just made sense, because he was doing fuck all to help Stilwell, and they even knew it in Washington. No wonder Mao kicked his ass over into Taiwan after the war. Sad part for the Chinese, they just exchanged an indifferent prick for a ruthless prick.

Now, Madame Chiang, his wife, she was the brains of the outfit, and that was one classy broad. None of us really had much respect for him, but his money was good when it was paid. Madame Chiang really took an interest in us and our welfare. She spoke great English and was a very polite lady. I have to say old Chiang married his ass up on that deal. They offered drinks, and I was reminded that Chennault still had spies on me. I said screw it and drank anyway.

And then I had another problem when I was accused of breaking into the bar and stealing liquor. They could not prove it. They even searched my quarters and found nothing, but I was accused anyway. Olga came up to me and said that I should just pay back the cost of the booze, and I told her they owed me money, and even if I did it, screw them. I told her that I would resign, and she said that they would hold that against me. I did not care; I was done with them, and they were sure as hell done with me. "Fuck them," I said.

I always got a lot of questions about the blood chits and our jackets. Those things became famous after the war. Those blood chits were made of silk. The chits identified the bearer as a friend of the Chinese. They asked the Chinese people to protect and help downed American flyers, and most did, hoping to get paid. Others would just ignore you—it was part of the culture. If they saved you, then they were responsible for you, and these were the poorest people on earth. They just did not need that shit, I guess. You had to feel sorry for them. They had to look at a future living in shit under the Kuomintang and Chiang, oppression under the communists, or slavery under the Japanese. If they had no water buffalo, they had no livelihood, because no rice meant no future. And in many Chinese minds, if there were no Americans, they had no hope.

Now that America was officially at war, we all knew that we were going to return to active duty, but most of us decided that when we did, it would be on our own terms, not Chennault's. Well, the days of the AVG were coming to an end anyway, so I took off and eventually boarded a ship and arrived in New York Harbor in July. I caught a train straight for DC and placed a letter of reinstatement, citing my agreement with Nimitz. I was told to go home and await orders, so I did.

After a few months I went back to my job of parking cars, the same job I had in college. I later learned that my orders were delayed due to a personal grudge someone held. All ten of us former Marines who fought with the AVG were in the same boat. In November [1942], I sent an express letter demanding a resolution to the problem, and three days later, I was ordered to San Diego. Well, I checked in, received my orders, left "Dego," and went to the South Pacific.

[On the TV series Baa Baa Black Sheep, later renamed Black Sheep Squadron:] Oh, the whole damned thing was Hollywood, but I guess that's showbiz. Yes, there was a Brigadier General James Moore, chief of staff of the 1st Marine Aircraft Wing [of Marine Air Group II], and he was a real stand-up guy. He took care of us and kept "Lard" [Lieutenant Colonel Joseph Smoak, operations officer of Marine Air Group II] off our backs. Now Smoak was a pain in the ass, a by-the-book Marine, but unlike most of the characteristic backstabbers, he would tell you to your face if he had a problem. He had served as a mud Marine in China, and I respected him for that. I was simply the kind of officer he could not stand. I had a lot of that in my career, so he was not unique.

When I hit Espiritu Santo, I became assistant operations officer. In May 1943, I was chosen by Elmer Brackett to be his executive officer for VMF-222, and I checked out in the [Chance] Vought F4U-1 Corsair. But as fate would have it, he was promoted and left, leaving me with the command. During my tenure there, I never even saw a Japanese aircraft. I did have a run-in with a naval pilot, some lieutenant commander who made some smart-ass comment about the Flying Tiger jacket I was wearing. I asked him if he liked his drink, because it would be about all he could eat for a few weeks when I beat the shit out of him. He said he would have me on charges. I told him to get in line. He was small-fry, and I had just pissed on a brigadier general. He left rather quickly.

I was stuck in operations and then moved into the S-2 [Intelligence] while I was on Guadalcanal awaiting permanent orders. When I arrived there we were told to always be on the alert because there were still Japanese hiding out on the island. One had been killed before I got there. I was called in and met some of the Army and other Marine guys. They had just finished up fighting for that island. Joe Foss became a living legend there, as did Marion Carl. Those guys really mixed it up with the Japs.

The P-38s were on Guadalcanal with us, and they had been ordered to make the intercept due to their range and speed. We helped plan the trip for them, and I told the men not to say anything. We did not want the Japs to know that we had broken their new code. However, soon Naval Intelligence was interrogating everyone on the island. Word of the mission had leaked out. I spoke with Rex Barber and Tom Lanphier, as they both claimed [Isoroku] Yamamoto on that mission. They still bitch about that shit. [*Barber was later given the official credit.*]

At this point my flying career was almost ruined when I broke my ankle in a football game and I was sent to Auckland, New Zealand, to recuperate. [*The other version was that he was injured wrestling on the barracks floor. (Tillman, note to author, March 25, 2021)*] I was worried that if they had to operate or put pins or some shit in it, I was done as a pilot. I got lucky, just a cast. I found out that not long after I left that VMF-222 scored thirty kills against the Japs. I guess they were waiting for me to leave. After I healed up, I was bounced from one squadron to another, although always in a no-flying status.

One of my jobs was to process the disciplinary paperwork of certain officers and enlisted men. I read through a lot of the charge sheets and I could not believe the bullshit I was reading. Guys were being brought up on charges for being out of uniform or missing roll call, and one guy, a lieutenant, was referred for court-martial because he brought an unauthorized pet kangaroo back from Australia. No shit. I thought that was pretty interesting, since in Burma we had a leopard. I guess the brass would have totally lost their shit if I had brought that thing with me on a leash. We actually used the story about the kangaroo in the TV show. I just could not believe how much time, energy, and paperwork was being used up on this bullshit. I guess life in the rear was boring, so they had to find a way to keep busy.

This was where I got the idea to try and form a squadron. I spoke to the MAG 11 commander, Colonel Lawson Sanderson, who gave his off-the-record approval, and I went to work collecting pilots wherever I could find them. Not all of these men were fighter pilots, but anyone could be converted, or so I thought. Unfortunately, Sanderson rotated out and "Lard" entered the scene. Well, the only thing left to do was to choose a squadron name.

This was a colorful group of guys. One of the men suggested "Boyington's Bastards" and I liked it, but I knew that would not fly. Another guy suggested "Devil's Dickheads." I suggested "Black Sheep," since we were not the typical, picture-perfect material glossing the magazines of the day. The name stuck, as did my two nicknames, "Gramps" and "Pappy," due to my age. I was about six to eight years older than most fighter pilots, which is sometimes regarded as a disadvantage. But I brought skill, tactical knowledge, and experience into it, and there were several pilots flying who were older than me.

We had just arrived in the Russell Islands. We had twenty Corsairs broken into five flights to escort 150 [Douglas SBD] Dauntless and [Grumman TBF] Avenger bombers on a mission to Ballale, near Bougainville. We ran into a heavy cloud base, lost sight of the bombers, and dropped below the clouds to try and pick them up. Sure enough, I saw the bombers doing their stuff on time and on target. However, just then we were jumped by forty Zeros with full fuel tanks. And these guys were no fools, or so I thought. I had Mo Fischer on my wing and he called them out.

One of them pulled up next to me, waggled his wings as if telling me to form up; then he pulled ahead. I had forgotten to turn on the gunsight or arm the guns, but when I did, I knocked him down. Mo blasted one off my tail, and we headed for the deck to protect the bombers. I nailed another one really quick, but I flew through the explosion. I saw another skimming the water trying to get away, so I chased him. I was closing on him when a little voice warned me, and I pulled away. There was his wingman. The lead guy had been the bait, and I had almost fallen for it. I turned in to the second Zero head-on. We closed in firing on each other, and I won.

The first Zero had disappeared, but I saw another coming head-on at lower altitude, and I got him, too. As I looked at the fuel gauge, I tried to milk my remaining fuel, and then I saw a Corsair just over the water and vulnerable being attacked by two Zeros. The Marine aircraft was damaged with oil all over the windscreen and was losing speed. I attacked the nearest Zero, and as I fired, he pulled up. I tried to follow him, still firing, and he broke apart, but I stalled out. I recovered enough to hit the second Zero and then I calmed down.

The adrenaline rush of air combat is something that you can't explain. I did not see the Corsair again or even know who was in it at the time, but Bobby Ewing was the only loss we had, so it must have been him. There was no way I could make it back to base, so I headed for Munda, where I made a perfect dead-stick landing, no gas at all. The loss of Ewing was a hard blow to the unit because he was very popular. He used to go coconut hunting with John Bolt. Bolt took it pretty hard also; they were best friends. Bolt and [Ed] Olander took Ewing under their wing, and Bolt had the most hours in the Corsair of any pilot in the squadron.

Yeah, we missed Bobby. That night I broke out a bottle of twenty-year-old scotch and we all had a shot in his honor. Then I had to write the letter to his family. Writing those letters is the hardest part of being a CO [commanding officer]. You do not want to just write a form letter, some generic shit that could belong to anybody. I always wrote each one on the specific pilot, attributing his characteristics, et cetera. I often wondered what would be written about me if I went down. "We regret to inform you that due to a night of drinking, your son, or husband, or what the hell ever, failed to return from a mission. He was last seen chasing some skirt down the slot disguised as an enemy aircraft." I could see it now! [*Laughs.*]

I scored five kills in one mission, and I would never do that again. Most of a combat pilot's missions are mundane and almost boring, especially when you are beginning to win a war and you outnumber the enemy. Our success appeased many of my naysayers, Smoak excepted. He had heard about the drinking problems in China and Burma, so he placed me on parole of sorts. I was not to drink, and if I did, I was to be reported. I still had a few, and he found out about it and put me in hack. Shortly after our first great success, I was invited along with my executive officer to the new commander's office and offered a drink. He assured me he was not part of Smoak's program, that I was safe.

Well, we soon got stuck with escort missions galore. We did not engage a single enemy plane in weeks, although the guys at Munda were having a hell of a time. They were the first line of defense. We finally got creative, especially when the Japs began to identify me over the radio. They would ask my position in plain English, although they were fooling no one. One day I gave them a lower altitude as a response, and sure enough, there came thirty Zeros. We caught sight of the Japs heading to twenty thousand feet to intercept us, but we were at twenty-five thousand feet, and we peeled over into them. We screamed into the enemy head-on, and I think everyone got a hit or a kill on the first pass.

My first hit blew up, and a second plane I hit began to smoke and the pilot bailed out. I continued to pull around and caught a third Jap, who also went down. We had done good work, and I was proud of my boys. We had scored twelve kills without a loss. I have to say that we had some great pilots, good guys all around, like Ed Olander, John Bolt, Bob McClurg, Hank McCartney, Bill Case, [Paul] "Moon" Mullen, Chris Magee, Bob Hanson, and others. They were all very sharp guys.

Sure, we had close calls, but most of my problems were caused less by the Japanese than by our own ground crews. Once I scrambled with the squadron to intercept some inbound enemy bombers, and in the middle of the dogfight with escorting Zeros, my engine died. I took a dive for the deck with a dozen meatballs on my ass. If it were not for the Navy pilots in a [Grumman F6F-3] Hellcat unit, I would not be here now. I headed back to base without fuel. My plane had not been refueled after the previous mission. That really pissed me off to the point I wanted to hurt somebody. I had had a perfect chance to score some bomber kills, and it was gone. [*Tillman comments: "When I was secretary of the Aces Association, one of the F6F pilots, Ken Hildebrandt VF-33, who had been land-based in the Solo-*

mons, said Boyington was describing a victory just after combat when a very wet, very cranky New Zealand P-40 pilot sloshed in. 'Who just shot down a single-engine fighter over Segi Point?' Boyington perked up: 'Can you confirm it for me?' SMACK! Kiwi laid him out with one punch. Leaned over and said, 'Next time, Yank, check recognition!' Turned about and sloshed out. Segi Point is on New Georgia and does not show in any of Boyington's credited victories." (Note to author, March 25, 2021)]

Another time I took off and the engine cowling tore loose, forcing me to return to the strip. Upon landing, I jumped into another Corsair and continued the mission but without any success. I never scored a bomber kill. But we did destroy a large number of aircraft on the ground during fighter-bomber and strafing missions. You can bet your sweet ass I had some very up-close and personal discussions with those ground crews. I walked in, called the maintenance chief over, chewed them out so loudly [Hideki] Tojo might have been interrupted back home. I then took my rank off and said, "Out-fucking-side now." I solved that problem.

We also did a few escorts for the Army Air Corps, and Ed Olander scored his fifth kill on that mission sometime in October, I think [October 17, 1943]. Once I chewed his ass because he was behind a Zero that was chasing me and he held his fire. He did not know who was in my Corsair, and he was afraid of hitting the friendly fighter. Once we hit the ground, I told him, "Don't worry about my ass, or anyone else's, just knock the bastards down."

I told them I was holding them all responsible until I saw the maintenance and refueling logs. I have never been the kind of guy to want to court-martial anyone due to my own personal record, but I was not there to do paperwork. I told them I was there to kick some motherfucker's ass, so step up, one at a time, and I will deal with each of them one at a goddamned time, just line the hell up and stand the fuck by. They knew my ass was serious. No one took me up on the challenge, but I was handed the logs, and saw who was responsible. That was the only time in my career I ever did paperwork to court-martial anyone, two guys who just got sloppy lazy. But it could have cost me my life and I am rather partial to it.

[Admiral William "Bull"] Halsey [Jr.] and some other brass came to see me at Munda and I liked him very much. He was just a quiet, well-spoken guy. He did not act like he was a four-star god lauding [lording it] over his peasants, not like [General Douglas] MacArthur and Chennault. He asked relevant questions, and you could tell that he was very interested in the answers. He had this scribe with him who wrote everything down. He inquired as to readiness, maintenance, what we needed, all that good stuff. Soon, maybe about two weeks later, we actually started getting new carburetors, points, plugs, magnetos, all the stuff that we were so short on to keep flying.

Now [Lewis B.] "Chesty" [Puller], on the other hand, was sort of like me ten times over and on steroids. He was one hell of a

Marine, the best Marine who ever served, probably. He was one of those few men I would have done anything for, because he cared about his men and loved the Corps. He had five Navy Crosses in his career [and one Army Distinguished Service Cross], and my understanding was that he never received the Medal of Honor due to politics. He did make three stars, but for him that was monumental.

I met him again many years later during Vietnam, and he was pissed that they would not let him go after he retired. When I asked him how he felt about being recommended a few times for the Medal of Honor, he just said, "It's not about the medals; it's all about the body count. As long as you can count a hell of a lot more of their dead than yours, and you achieved your objective, then you did your job." What a guy.

Contrary to what I have heard over the years, I was stone-cold sober the day of the flight [when Boyington was shot down], which was January 3, 1944. Everything started out wrong that day. My plane was down, so I had to take another. I led the squadron on a fighter sweep to Rabaul. Everyone knew that I was expected to beat Joe Foss's record of twenty-six kills, since he had just tied Eddie Rickenbacker's score not long before. Even Marion Carl allowed me the opportunity to lead several of his flights, giving me the chance to increase my score. He is a great guy. This was because I was due to be rotated out due to age and longevity. Probably also because I had pissed off all the wrong people. At this time, I had twenty-five [*Boyington was officially credited with twenty-one victories*] and Rabaul was just about the best hunting ground you could imagine.

Well, to make a long story short, my wingman George Ashmun [KIA on this mission] and I were looking for trouble, and George just told me to focus on getting the kills, that he would take care of my six. Soon we were surrounded, and I scored three kills, but George was overwhelmed, and I was trying to help him when I was also hit. I could feel and hear the shells striking the armor plate and fuselage. Twenty-millimeter cannon rounds make a loud bang, whereas the 7.7 bullets make a *ping-ping* sound. I heard a lot of bangs. I remember my body being tossed around, and suddenly I had a fire in the cockpit. The engine and fuel line had been shot up, I guess. I could smell the gas.

I was about a hundred feet above the water, so I did not have much choice. George had already been flamed and hit the ocean. I was apparently going to share the same fate, so I managed to kick out of the Corsair and pull the rip cord. I felt a hard jerk and I was instantly in the water. After I hit the water, I managed to inflate my rubber raft, but my Mae West was shot full of holes and was no good. I assessed my injuries, saw that I was beyond screwed up, and hoped that I would be rescued. That wish became urgent once four Zero pilots began taking turns strafing me in the water.

A few hours later a Jap submarine on the way to Rabaul surfaced and collected me. I assumed they had been vectored by the fighters, perhaps one had a radio. I dumped everything of military value over the side. I was hurting. Well, I nearly lost my left ear, which was hanging in a bloody mess. My scalp had a massive laceration, my arms, groin, and shoulders were peppered with shrapnel, and a bullet had gone through my left calf. Luckily, the sub crew tried to take care of me. They were very humane, and I wondered if this was the type of treatment I could expect in the future. One of the crew spoke English and assured me that I was going to be all right.

I was totally unprepared [for capture]. I believe that even if we had been prepared for captivity and interrogation, we would have still been unprepared to some extent, since we would have trained our men in the Occidental method of psychological warfare and interrogation resistance.

[Imprisonment] was hard. We were beaten on occasion and questioned about even the most ridiculous bullshit. Most of the guards were pretty brutal, but once you learned how to out-think them, you could get by. They often withheld food as a form of torture, and they would always bring in an English speaker to ask the same dumb-ass questions. For most, I had no clue what they were talking about.

There was this old lady in Japan whom I worked for in the kitchen at the camp. By the time I got there, I was down sixty or seventy pounds and not looking so good. She took care of me, and I owe her as much as anyone. However, despite the beatings and starvation diet, I probably lived as long as I have due to the fact that twenty months in prison prevented me from drinking.

The one exception was New Year's Eve 1944, when a guard gave me some sake. Another important person was Mr. Kono, a mysterious man who spoke English and wore a uniform without rank. He perhaps did more to save American lives than anyone else.

As far as holding a grudge, no. I never did that. I figured the people were just as much a victim as we were. Their government was in control and the population was not like ours. There was no great mindset of revolution or overthrowing their regime. That was not their way. The Japanese civilians who had been bombed out were always around us showing respect. Many of them went out of their way to help us at great risk to themselves, slipping us food. Basically, just showing us kindness.

I think that was because of a few things. Their humanity came through, they saw how bad it was for us, and they probably felt ashamed. Deep in their minds, they knew they had started this shit, and they were now reaping the benefits of a fucked-up emperor and a military dictatorship. I also think that despite the Jap propaganda machine spewing victory after victory, even the most limited Japanese mind knew their shit was getting weaker by the day and they were going to lose the war.

[Tillman calls Boyington's account a "rare perspective on POW relations with guards and civilians" and could not "recall hearing such details about sympathetic civilians" previously. (Note to author, March 18, 2021) My interview with American POW and Doolittle raider Chase Nielsen (captured April 18, 1942) also challenges Boyington's interpretation of the POW-civilian relationship, al-

though Nielsen did have limited contact with civilians. (I inter-viewed Nielsen several times by phone, and in person on April 17 and 18, 2002.) In addition, Fred Turnbull, a retired Navy 0-6 (cap-tain) and former Hellcat pilot in the same POW camp in Japan, related a far different account courtesy of Barrett Tillman: "From the start it was obvious that even the Japanese looked on him as some kind of celebrity POW. Boyington had been shipped in from some other camp. . . . While thin, he was not emaciated like Fred and the others. . . . Almost immediately they were surprised when Boyington was assigned to work in the Japanese officers' kitchen. No other POW had ever worked there. A nice elderly lady was the chief cook, and one thing became very apparent. . . . While all the other POWs were starving to death . . . Greg Boyington was gain-ing weight! Fred and others had actually risked their lives to escape at night and steal vegetables from nearby fields to try and keep those too weak to walk, alive. . . . The camp seniors . . . confront[ed] Boyington and encourage[d] him to try to steal some food for the very weak, since he obviously had special access: some meat here, rice or vegetables there . . . anything to help the starving. Boyington flat-out refused! Too risky . . . He had a good deal and wasn't go-ing to do anything to screw it up. Over time, he was approached by many to please help. . . . Each time he refused. While Boyington was being hailed as a hero in the United States . . . he was being shunned by his fellow POWs with utter contempt. (Tillman, email to author, March 25, 2021)]

We managed to stay updated on the war news, especially thanks to friendly guards who would tell us what was going on.

Of course, you never knew if what they said was true; you had to assess each man as you came to know him. I picked up the Japanese language pretty quickly, and I could understand many phrases and key words. New prisoners were also a great source of information. But I was informed by a Japanese man that Roosevelt had died and that Germany had surrendered. Later we were moved from Ōfuna to a real POW camp. This was a great thing, because we were up to that point below prisoner status. At least when we were POWs, our families could hear that we were alive and reasonably well. That also meant that it would be more difficult for the Japs to just execute us with no one asking questions, which was always on our minds. [*Tillman recalls meeting a visitor to the Hook in the early eighties who was on PacFleet staff when Boyington was shot down. Tillman has "long forgotten" the man's name, but remembers his message as follows: "SigInt had picked up Pappy's trail. Gent said that crypto decoded a message from the RADM at Truk, requesting Tokyo's permission to execute a field-grade USMC officer—might have said Boyington. Anyway, there was no doubt of the POW's ID. The former staffer said his boss immediately realized the implications, knowing GB had been recommended for the MoH. 'Let us hope that the good admiral's request is granted.' Something to the effect that it would spare everybody a good deal of trouble." (Note to author, March 21, 2021)*]

As soon as we were moved to a more solid structure, I felt a little better, especially once the Boeing B-29 raids picked up the pace. We would see them at high altitude, sometimes engaged by a Jap, but they just gave us so much hope. I think that was the biggest factor in the Japs treating us better. They knew it was not going to end in their favor.

However, once the bombing picked up, we were placed on rubble-clearing details and digging tunnels in the hills. This was near Yokohama. One bit of irony was when a guard told me about a single bomb that had been dropped on his home in Nagasaki. It was not until after I was released that I found out it was true. In September I also found out from a guard that the war was over. The guards almost to a man got drunk at the news, and some were openly discussing killing us. Another guard had said that it would be a bad idea, since the Americans would come, and he just wanted to go home.

Six days later I was standing in front of the Swiss Red Cross in new quarters and very clean. A few days later the B-29s were dropping food and clothes to us, and a few guys were killed by being hit by packages. Soon the Navy landed with the Marines, and we were able to leave. We went to the hospital ship *Benevolence*, where the medical staff checked us all out, and I had the best meal in memory, ham and eggs.

The media hype started almost immediately, as soon as I was on the ship. I didn't really have much to say, except hello to my family. After I was cleared, I flew from Tokyo to Guam, Kwajalein, and Pearl Harbor, headed stateside. Major General [James] Moore met me at Pearl Harbor and gave me the use of his quarters, a car and driver, which was great. I had decided to change my ways, accept my fate, and clean myself up. I felt that if the nation was going to honor me as a hero, I should honor the nation by acting like one. But as I have often said, "Show me a hero and I'll show you a bum."

[*Heroes and bums: according to Tillman, the truth of this statement was definitively brought home in an encounter between Boyington and Fred Turnbull. Turnbull stopped "dead in his tracks" when he, Harry Gann, and Tillman discovered Boyington "sitting at a table selling autographed copies of* Baa Baa Black Sheep *at the Reno Air Races. Fred hesitated for only a few seconds and then . . . walked right up to Boyington. When Boyington saw him, he had a surprised look on his face . . . [and] quietly said, 'Hello, Fred . . . how have you been?' From where I was standing, I could see Fred's neck turning red. . . . He was almost shaking. He looked down and said (I'll never forget this), 'You're here signing books and all these idiots think you're a hero. But I know the truth. You're one of the most despicable human beings I've ever known!' Boyington never said another word. He sheepishly . . . turned and walked into the RV parked behind him. Fred then muttered something, turned, and . . . said, 'I'm sorry, guys, but I hate that son of a bitch more than anyone else in this world.'" (Email to author, March 25, 2021)*]

In San Francisco, twenty of the guys had shown up, remembering that we had planned on a party six months after the war was over, and they decided to have one then and there. For PR purposes I did these war bond drives with Frank Walton, the S-2 of the squadron. We talked to people all over the country, but I still had not received my back pay. I was just living off the generosity of others, broker than hell.

When we went to Washington, DC, I received the Navy Cross

from [Major] General Alexander [Archer] Vandegrift [USMC, Medal of Honor], the commandant [of the United States Marine Corps]. Then I went to see President Harry S. Truman, who gave me the big one [Medal of Honor]. After that it was a New York ticker-tape parade, then more traveling. Later I was retired due to wounds, but that only made things worse. I could not find a job until I began working as a wrestling referee part-time. My second wife, Fanny, kept me out of too much trouble. Later I was a beer salesman for a few years; it seemed like poetic justice in a way. It made me sober up again after falling off the wagon. Well, I sobered up after a bad crash and burn once—it happens. We still have reunions of the AVG and Black Sheep, and Dick Rossi handles all the AVG gatherings.

We had some great reunions, and it was good to see the old faces. Sometimes I will see a guy who I have not seen since the war, and that is true with Flying Tiger and Black Sheep reunions. I go to the Medal of Honor gatherings, where I always see Doolittle, Foss, Howard, and a bunch of the old gang. I once had a drinking contest with Audie Murphy and he lost, but I liked him. He still looked like a kid.

[*In one of his interviews with me, Joe Foss had a less-than-fond memory of meeting up with Boyington at one such reunion. Tillman also recalls hearing Foss recount the encounter at Medal of Honor and other veterans' events: "Boyington got a snoot full and wanted to wrestle. Joe was a good six feet tall and pretty well-built, but he said Boyington was strong as a bull and could not be stopped physically. Boyington shoved him against a pillar and Joe's head*

collided—he said he saw stars. Finally, he got an arm free and clob-
bered Boyington with a fist. Time passed. Much later Boyington
knocked on Joe's door and said something like 'We sure had fun,
didn't we?'" (Note to author, March 26, 2021)]

I don't think a man, let alone an officer, could get away with
the things we used to pull back then. And that is probably not
a bad thing. The wars that followed were pretty much like any
other. I think that our government should be more particular as
to which wars we get involved in. I think that as long as we
never lose focus on what's important, we will be all right.

Postscript

Gregory Boyington's bad-boy image was greatly enhanced (or
exacerbated) by the 1970s television pilot *The Flying Misfits*,
which later became the series *Baa Baa Black Sheep* (later renamed *Black Sheep Squadron*), starring Robert Conrad as Boyington. Other Black Sheep I interviewed said that they cringed
at the show's historical inaccuracies and outright abrogation of
logic. According to Ed Olander, "If they had done a series about
the real Black Sheep, it would have lasted one season and been
the most boring show in history. They shot down more planes
in one season on that show than we shot down during the entire war. I was very impressed, since I did not think we were
that good."

John Bolt put it more ironically: "I wished I could have been
on that set every day to watch all the nurses and shenanigans
going on, to see what I had apparently missed out on. But there

were some accuracies to the show. There were Corsairs, there were Marines, there were Japanese pilots, and there was a war. Other than that, there was no resemblance to reality." To sum up in the words of General Bruce Matheson: "Well, if we'd had Quonsets instead of flooded tents, decent chow, all that booze, AND NURSES—hell, I'd still be out there!"

Bolt nevertheless held Boyington in high esteem: "Greg was not a perfect man, far from it. But he was a leader who cared about his men, and he led from the front, by example, and that is just about the best that you could expect from any combat leader. The rest is just human frailty." Most of the Flying Tigers who flew with Boyington, however, were not as forgiving of his personal flaws. Brigadier General David Lee "Tex" Hill described him as "quite a guy, and the only man I ever knew who could stretch the truth until it needed surgery." Hill also said, "Boyington lives in his own world, and it must be a very lonely place. It is OK to visit him there. Just do not take up residence." Brigadier General James Howard commented, "If bullshit artist was a military occupational specialty, Boyington would have been at the top of the promotion list. Take what he tells you with a pound of salt. However, he is very entertaining, unless he is drunk. Then you just want to get the hell away from him."

Dick Rossi's opinions of Boyington were also mixed, at best. Rossi called him "a good pilot," but said, "He made some of us nervous because he did not always fly sober, and he was out for personal glory, not really a team player." Charles Older, too, voiced serious reservations: "Boyington would be the first guy I would want with me killing Japs, but the last guy I would put on the stand under oath." Colonel Ed Rector was downright dismissive: "The only thing Boyington killed with any efficiency were many bottles of booze."

Brigadier General Joseph Foss, Boyington's fellow Medal of Honor recipient and Marine Corps fighter ace, had his own mixed critique: "Greg was a shameless exhibitionist who had little respect for authority or the rules. He just did not think they applied to him. To be honest, I had very little use for him personally. I think he was an embarrassment to the Corps. But he was a very effective combat pilot and a good leader to his men. That's the best I can really say about him."

★　★　★

I'd like to thank my friend and fellow author Barrett Tillman, one of our very finest aviation historians, for his valuable contributions to this chapter on Boyington. Barrett knew that I would be including controversial and seemingly contradictory information if I could obtain documentation, and he generously offered to relay a significant amount of previously unpublished material regarding Boyington's life and the judgment of his peers that I had heard about but never before corroborated.

One incident that Barrett recounted seems especially fitting to close this portrait of Boyington. "Fred [Turnbull], Harry Gann, and myself were in Pensacola. Close to midnight, Fred called our rooms and demanded we meet him immediately in the bar. I got dressed and met Harry at the elevator. We go down and walk into the bar and Fred already had our scotches lined up. To that point we had no idea what was going on. We picked up our drinks and Fred holds his up like a toast and announces: 'My life is complete! I outlived the son of a bitch!' He then points to the TV, which was on mute. The scrawl was announcing that World War II Marine hero 'Pappy' Boyington had just died." (Note to author, March 25, 2021)

As I said to Barrett, "I will not write a hagiography about anyone, including Boyington. The interview is what it is, but warts and all, it will be the story." The good, the bad, and the ugly are now all part of the published Boyington saga. Boyington had his demons. I hope he is at peace with them. I leave it to readers and fellow historians to sift through the debris of what was his remarkable life.

MEDAL OF HONOR CITATION

Major Gregory Boyington, USMC

For extraordinary heroism above and beyond the call of duty as Commanding Officer of Marine Fighting Squadron TWO FOURTEEN in action against enemy Japanese forces in Central Solomons Area from September 12, 1943, to January 3, 1944. Consistently outnumbered throughout successive hazardous flights over heavily defended hostile territory, Maj. Boyington struck at the enemy with daring and courageous persistence, leading his squadron into combat with devastating results to Japanese shipping, shore installations and aerial forces. Resolute in his efforts to inflict crippling damage on the enemy, Maj. Boyington led a formation of twenty-four fighters over Kahili on October 17, and, persistently circling the airdrome where 60 hostile aircraft were grounded, boldly challenged the Japanese to send up planes. Under his brilliant command, our fighters shot down 20 enemy craft in the ensuing action without the loss of a single ship. A superb airman and determined fighter against overwhelming odds, Maj. Boyington personally destroyed 26 of the many Japanese planes shot down by his squadron and by his forceful leadership developed the combat readiness in his command which was a distinctive factor in the Allied aerial achievements in this vitally strategic area.

Harry S. Truman, October 4, 1945

BRIGADIER GENERAL
JOSEPH JACOB FOSS, USMC (RET.)

APRIL 17, 1915–JANUARY 1, 2003

In the hundreds of interviews that I've conducted with veterans of many conflicts around the world, several stand out not for their awards and decorations, nor even for their incredible combat service, but because they simply excel in everything they do, both in and out of uniform. Joe Foss is one of these. All of Foss's twenty-six victories were in the service of the United States Marine Corps, and all twenty-six were verified. He thus is entitled to claim the title of leading Marine Corps ace, a title erroneously held by Greg Boyington.

Joe Foss never did anything halfway. He was a bull charging forward, clearing a path and blazing trails. A gifted fighter pilot, he was also a true cowboy who would have felt just as at home in the Old West with a six-shooter on his hip, riding a horse while herding cattle or even clearing a saloon in a bar fight.

The major impression everyone had after speaking with Foss was that he was as genuine as anyone could possibly be. Either you liked and respected Foss, or you feared and avoided him for his bluntness: he did not hold back, could spot a fake a mile away, and never shrank from controversy if he felt the cause was just. In many aspects, he was much like his friend Major General Marion Carl; there was no pretense, no bluster, no arrogance or self-aggrandizing about Foss. His word was good: when he gave it, he kept it, no further discussion needed. Joe Foss was also a very affable, congenial man with a great heart full of compassion for the less fortunate. He was a man of religious faith, and his political beliefs and worldview could send liberals into inpatient therapy.

Most of our discussions took place by phone from 1986 through the late 1990s. We last spoke very shortly before the terror attacks on September 11, 2001. On the two occasions I met with him in person, he proved to be a great guy to be around. He was not one for idle small talk, but if you brought up a subject that was of interest to him, his depth of knowledge was often breathtaking. His opinions were his own, but they came from a wealth of experience. As a historian, I could not hope for a better interview subject.

Foss and other veterans, especially World War II fighter pilots, often had contentious relationships with Gregory Boyington. Most of the other pilots respected Boyington's record and achievements, but did not respect the man. Foss was of the opinion that Boyington's conduct during his captivity and his postwar behavior tarnished the Marine Corps and the Medal of Honor. He was very clear about his opinions and why he held them, but he was reserved in his condemnation. "Boyington had to live with himself," he said. "I expect that it must have been a very lonely place. I actually felt sorry for him." And he was not alone in that assessment.

As I've said before, the best measure of a warrior is to gather the opinions of his peers, and, if possible, those of his enemies. Foss's peers all had the same opinion of him, summed up by Marion Carl: "If you had to get into a fight, then Joe was the guy you wanted on your wing. Yes, he was fearless, determined, and focused in combat. But he never threw pragmatism out the window or pushed a bad position to get a kill if it meant risking a single member of his flight. That is a real leader, and that, basically, is Joe Foss." Imperial Japanese Navy ace Saburō Sakai described Joe Foss as "a good man and a true American hero," and "a man that I am happy to call my friend."

Warrior, businessman, politician, television personality, outdoorsman, cowboy, humanitarian, intellectual: all of these terms fit Joe Foss well. Highly talented, skilled, and of irreproachable conduct, he is perhaps best of all described by the broadcaster Lowell Thomas: "Joe Foss, in the South Pacific air war, established himself as the American ace of aces. Joe Foss, when he returned to the United States to receive the Congressional Medal of Honor, impressed those who met him as the perfect fighting man, the instinctive and relentless hunter. . . . Tall, handsome, modest, he is the embodiment of the frontiersman of old, the stalker of game, the trailer of human enemies."

JOE FOSS

I was born on April 17, 1915. A South Dakota kid, I grew up on a farm, plowing and taking care of the animals, doing the usual farm things. My dad's family came from Bergen, Norway, as immigrants and settled in Minnesota. There seems to be a great attraction to that state for Scandinavians—Norwegians, Danes, and Swedes. It's almost like a damned Viking colony. It makes sense of how the Minnesota Vikings football team got their name.

But I always loved the idea of flying. Almost every boy of my generation who became a pilot had the same thoughts. I was enthralled by flying, watching the mail pilots as they flew overhead. They were gods to me.

When Charles Lindbergh flew across the Atlantic, I was twelve years old. That spark I had to fly was reignited big-time. Dad was also interested in flying, and we read everything we could get on the subject—magazines, books, you name it. When Lindbergh came back to the States, he went on a cross-country tour. Dad found out he was going to be in Sioux Falls, and we had to go. On the big day, we dressed up and drove to Renner Field about five miles out of town. I was so excited, I climbed up on the platform, but these uniformed guys threw me off.

Well, with that hope of meeting him dashed, I went to inspect his plane. On the way home I told Dad about my new dream, and he seemed to support it. As time went on, he actually endorsed my enthusiasm. Many years later Charles Lindbergh would become a close personal friend.

We were a pretty traditional immigrant family. My dad assimilated easily, except where his name was concerned. He really hated the name Olouse, so he went by Frank to blend in. He was used to a life of hard work. He and his brother, my uncle Martin, were boxers and wrestlers—good at it, too—and had traveled with a circus. But he was also highly intelligent and could fix things, and he was enchanted by gadgets and machines. Tractors, cars, electric things, it did not matter: if it was broken, he could usually fix it. He loved cars and started his own car dealership and repair business when they were living in Jaspar, Minnesota. We always had a decent car as a result.

My dad was perhaps the most talented man I ever knew. He could hitch and drive horses, plow like a madman, plant trees and crops, shoot a rifle like a sniper, and was very musically inclined, too. He played a fiddle and could carry a tune. My mother; younger brother, Cliff; and sister, Mary Flora, and I would just sing along. Dad taught all of us to ride a horse as soon as we were walking at a fast pace. That was our entertainment. There was no television back then and we did not have a radio, which was the big family entertainment back in those days. We lived a very simple life, not like today. I guess I inherited the musical gift from Dad because I took up the saxophone.

My mother and father met when he was working for the Great Northern Railway Company in 1914 as an engineer. He was not from a farming background, but my mother inherited land, about 160 acres, not a large farm really, and convinced him to drop the railroad job and take up farming. My Scottish-Irish mother was Catholic, and Dad was a Lutheran. Her name was Mary Lacey, and her family moved from New York. Her dad was a doctor, but he died not long after they settled several hundred acres near Sioux Falls. They were such different people in many ways.

Dad was very open and friendly. He thrived at a party and could do anything to entertain. He used to tell great stories, sometimes the same ones over and over. He was willing to shake anybody's hand, tell a joke. Mom was more reserved and private. Whereas Dad had a great sense of humor, Mom was—well, let's say, "lacking in the humor department." Dad was a Republican; Mom was a Democrat, so how those two ever got along, I have no idea. Both were hard workers, and Mom was as good on the farm as any man. She did it all, from milking to plowing to traditional housekeeping and cooking, but she preferred working the farm. She really was the perfect farm wife. My brother, Cliff, liked working the farm, but that was not what motivated me. I did not want to be a farmer. The sky was my real love.

We were a very patriotic family. Despite their political differences, my parents were hard-core Americans, make no mistake. And despite the religious differences, both had a strong belief in God. They made sure that we knew that and respected the Good Book. My dad always told me not to ever get involved with politics, because an honest politician was a rare bird and I would never make any money. Well, he was pretty right about that, but I did not listen. I ran for governor [of South Dakota] twice and won. I guess if you're just honest and try to do good, people will see that. If you are a selfish shit, people will see that also. I think Dad would have been proud of me.

Dad always told me that the only limits I had on my life were those I placed on myself. "Never let another man tell you that you can't do something. Do it and prove him wrong," he said. He also insisted on being honest and working hard, because both would bring rewards, and also respect from others. He also said that being generous was a blessing, but being a generous fool led to poverty. Be smart with money but be selectively charitable at the same time. My dad had a lot of business friends, some more, some less legitimate than others. Our Cadillac was bought from one of his buddies who was a bootlegger. This car would be called a "James Bond mobile" today. It could spray smoke and drop roofing nails if being chased, and it was fast. Dad had some interesting business associates.

I was an adventurous kid, always exploring, and when I got together with the other boys, we just did things that kids back then did. Exploring, fishing, never really getting into any real trouble. Once Mom caught me climbing up the windmill, and she was not really happy about that. If any of us were to get into trouble, we hoped Dad would be the administrator of justice, not Mom. Well, except the time I shot at an electric transformer. That got me into deep trouble with Dad, I can tell you. He knew what I'd done before I got home, so I confessed. I lost my gun privileges for a year as a result, so that taught me a valuable lesson.

Dad had taught me how to shoot because it came in handy. Dad had this Springfield rifle in .45-70, and after I learned on a Daisy BB gun, and later a Remington .22. We had a real varmint problem living out in the farm country. You name it—we probably had the critters. There were coyotes around that liked to go after our newborn calves. Dad dropped one coyote on the run, a kill shot, leading the target and adjusting for the range and light wind. Foxes would try to get the chickens, ducks, geese, any critter they could. We also had pigs, so the piglets were at risk unless they were enclosed well. We lost calves occasionally, and I hated that because we raised them and gave them names, and they were a very important part of our livelihood. Dad also put me in charge of hunting the many gophers that burrowed in the ground. This was a real problem for the horses and cows, because when they broke a leg, you had to put them down. I hated that. So I took the job, a nickel per gopher, so game on! I bagged a lot of gophers, I can tell you.

We had deer, elk, all kinds of wild critters that we hunted on occasion. Dad would take Cliff and me hunting for rabbits, and we went bird hunting quite often, mostly pheasants. One of our hunting buddies, an Army Air Corps officer named Nathan Twining, went on many hunts with us before I went off to college. We met again during the war, when he was one of the top generals in Army Air Corps, and later the Air Force.

Dad taught us that a hunter is a conservator. Kill what you need and will eat, never overhunt to affect the health of the herds, and respect the land and all living things. We also fished for food more than recreation. If it did not go on the table, there was no reason to kill it, unless it was a varmint threatening livestock. I always get amused by these liberal city slickers who moan about hunting. Trying to educate these people about animal population control and land management is like trying to paint a running river. It ain't gonna happen.

Bagging gophers, I learned the value of free-market capitalism. I also started trapping animals for money, along with doing odd jobs like working on the windmills at neighboring farms. Cleaning those windmills, bagging varmints, I did whatever I could do. When I was fifteen, I saved enough money to buy my first car, a convertible. I felt like a king. I could then drive to school, taking Cliff, Mary Flora, sometimes a few friends. My dad's rule was: straight to school and back afterward, unless I had an errand to run for him.

Well, two of my buddies joined me one day and convinced me to drive to another high school to see some girls they knew. I did not think my father would find out. It was not a long drive, and I would not be late for school. One of these guys, called Joe

Conger, was from that other high school. My cousin Jake and I met him when we snuck into the theater to see a movie for free. Joe was the usher and we became great friends. Ironically, we both joined the Marine Corps, went to flight school, and then were in the same unit flying together on Guadalcanal.

Well, as fate would have it, I was going through an intersection and clipped another car's rear bumper. Both cars lost bumpers—a repair job, nothing too bad. The guy got out mad as hell and asked for my telephone number. I offered to pay for the repair. He handed me his business card. As luck would have it, he was a damned lawyer. I threw the bumper in the back, and the entire day at school was misery for me. When I drove home, Dad was there with my uncle Frank. He told me to put the car away in the shed. I did and came back and gave him the keys.

That car would remain there until the start of the next school year, so I had to walk about six miles round trip to school and back, five days a week for the last couple of months. Dad drove my brother and sister to school, but I walked. That was my punishment. That also limited my summer activities, so I missed out on a lot. But I learned a valuable lesson: always do what you must do and obey the rules. And if you give your word, you keep it. My dad was not at all an abusive father, but he sure as hell knew how to teach you a lesson. I did get popped upside the head a few times. Mom did that usually, but I always earned it.

There was a bright side during the time I had to walk to and from school. My father and I took a ride in an airplane after I arrived home. When Dad and I drove to the field, the landing strip was lit by kerosene drums used as markers. When the Ford Tri-Motor landed, the pilot turned out to be a local legend, Clyde Ice. He owned an airline called *Wambler Ohanka*, or "Swift Eagle" in the Sioux language. We climbed aboard at a cost of $1.50 per person, which was a lot of money back then.

We were shown how to strap into our seat belts, and I looked out the window. I was as excited as hell, as you may imagine. After we landed, Dad and I watched a few more flights, and by the time we got home, my father had no doubt that I was going to become a pilot. A few things about that pilot. Clyde had over forty-three thousand hours of flight time in his career, which is probably still a world record. He never had a crash, injury, or fatality, and he amazingly flew into his early nineties. He died in 1992 at age 103, and was someone I called friend. He was just a good guy.

If that was not enough to sink the hook into me, a few weeks later, the Marine Corps exhibition flight team flew in for a show. They flew the open-cockpit F4B4 types, and they had four of them. Later I trained on those aircraft and came to know all four of those pilots when they were senior officers. I learned that Marine Corps aviation is indeed a very small world. Two years later I took another flight when my cousin and I flew with a barnstormer named Billeter. He flew a biplane, a two-seater, and gave rides. His plane was not exactly the airworthiest in appearance. That hooked me. I was going to be a pilot for sure.

But things can happen that just drop-kick you, you know?

Life can be very unfair, whether in peacetime or in war. A major rain and lightning storm rolled in one day when we were working at my uncle Frank's. I was taking the tractor to the barn, so my dad left, saying he would meet me at home. I parked the tractor out of the storm and was driving home when I saw Dad's car on the side of the road. I stopped and saw that he had been electrocuted by a downed electrical wire that touched the car. He was dead and there was nothing I could do. Another driver pulled up behind me and we pulled my dad away. I started artificial respiration, which I knew how to do, but it did no good. My world fell apart at that moment. He was really the glue in the family. That was the worst day of my life.

My mother took my dad's death really hard, but her stoic nature would not allow her to openly grieve. She just kept doing the best she could while Cliff and I threw our weight into making things work: plowing, fertilizing, harvesting, you name it. The work did not stop because Pop was gone. It just meant that there was more work to do. I was never a stellar student, and there was no danger of my becoming a scholar. I just knew that as soon as possible I wanted to leave that farm. But then I had a guilty conscience, knowing that would leave my mother struggling even more. I was torn between my dreams of flying and my obligation to the family.

Things became hard for us in many ways due to the Great Depression. Those with farm animals and crops would be expected to fare better, but we had a long drought that ruined farming. We had windstorms that just obliterated the topsoil all over the Midwest. This combination of events created John Steinbeck's masterpieces. He wrote about the times we were experiencing, and although they were fictionalized, everyone could relate to the characters in his books, which I read with a clear understanding. I was living it.

Despite my dismal high school performance, I enrolled in Augustana College in Sioux Falls. I had to earn the money for school, so I worked at a meatpacking plant. I also worked at the filling station, doing basic car work and pumping gas, and worked as a janitor at the church, and I still repaired those windmills on occasion. I even boxed and did pretty well in the ring. I won quite a few fights and tried for the Golden Gloves competition.

My first big fight was against this guy who knocked me down a lot. I ended up getting knocked out of the ring and landed on a press reporter's typewriter of all things. I did not have a clear recollection of how I got there—my bell had been rung a few times, and I had a broken nose. When that picture made the local paper, I decided that being a professional fighter was not really my calling. I spoke to Jimmy Doolittle about that a few times, as he had done the same thing. He was just better at it. He told me that he had to fight under an assumed name because his mother would have had a seizure if she knew he was fighting for money.

I even worked as a bouncer at an illegal casino. I was doing well for the time in the wages I was earning, but the hours were long, and I was always tired. My schoolwork suffered, and I was failing out. The dean suggested I stick to farming, so I left school. I still worked the other jobs and even picked the saxophone up and played with a band. That paid better than the other jobs combined, but I still wanted to fly.

The next big job was when Cliff, Mom, and I worked clearing roads of snow for the highway department. That was the winter of 1935–36, when the temperature dropped to forty below zero and sometimes even colder for long periods of time. We had cattle that got caught in snowdrifts and died. The snowfall was so bad many of the roads were closed because they were impassable. Wells froze—that was how cold it was. I was the oldest son, so by rights I would inherit the farm, but I wanted none of it. Cliff had finished high school, so we had a discussion. I told him it was all his when the time came. I had other plans.

I decided to go ahead and learn to fly, so I went over to the Sioux Falls airport and asked how much it would cost me. The amount, $64, was a lot of money, but I was making that at the filling station, so I knew I could do it.

I had this flight instructor who I will never forget named Roy Lanning. He had this Taylorcraft, a high-wing, closed-canopy plane like a Cessna 152 or 172 series of light planes today—well, sort of. I learned rather quickly and shortly did my first solo flight. As I was learning, I thought about my dad and how he would have been proud to be sitting next to me. I still think about him a lot, even all these years later. But even after passing the ground exams and flight tests, I still had to rent the plane to accumulate hours, and that was really expensive, about $6 an hour. I could not afford to get the required hours in a reasonable amount of time, so I decided to join the military. That would cost nothing.

Like most men my age, I stayed up-to-date on what was going on in Asia and Germany. There was trouble coming for someone. The Spanish Civil War exploded with the Russians and Germans each supporting their sides, Japan invaded China, and Hitler was in Austria and Czechoslovakia. I spoke about these events with my friends, and we all agreed that there was going to be a war, but we weren't sure if America would be involved. My argument was this: if Great Britain or France got dragged into a war, we would follow soon enough.

Even Lindbergh was quite vocal about the need for American airpower. I was well aware of what [Brigadier General William Lendrum] Billy Mitchell had gone through, fighting both the Army and the Navy. He proved them wrong as hell when he sank that battleship [Ostfriesland] from the air, making a statement that bombers would win wars and battleships had seen their day. That did not sit well with the entrenched Navy types, and the Army wanted his ass because he was fighting for that branch to have a separate air arm. Lindbergh supported that theory, as he saw the growing strength of Germany and Japan. He also became a big isolationist, warning us about getting involved in foreign conflicts, especially another European war.

Lindbergh was not alone; many people in this country believed that no European problems should become American problems. You have to also remember that a lot of recent immigrants from Italy and Germany living here still believed that Germany was treated badly after the First World War. They also believed that Britain and France only wanted to keep their respective empires together, and that meant problems with Japan also. The Belgians also had their own holdings in Africa, and there was no way Belgium would not be dragged into it. Hell, even I knew that. I read history and kept up with current events.

Then there was my mother stressing education again. I tried to get back into college, but the dean would not let me in, due to my poor performance. I then changed course and enrolled in Sioux Falls College. I still worked, played football, and ran track, and I began boxing again. My accommodations ended up being an attic converted to living space shared with two friends from high school, Herbie Creighton and Duane Tuttle. Money was still tight, but I knew I could make it if I was smart. I was still flying and getting my hours in.

After my first year, I had a B average, and I transferred to the University of South Dakota and joined the Sigma Alpha Epsilon fraternity. The school also had a military flight program. When I told my family that I planned on joining the military as a pilot, my mother went off. She demanded that I get a college degree. I decided to split the difference. I stayed in school and enlisted in the Army National Guard. It gave me an additional source of income and also made it easier to get into a military flight program later. I was assigned to the 147th Field Artillery. I made a lot of new friends, many of them aviation-minded like me.

The military life suited me. The discipline and routine, which I was sort of used to from working a farm, were OK with me. All of us knew a war was coming, and we managed to get a Civil Aeronautics Administration course started at the university. I thought it would look good if I had these courses under my belt. With more knowledge and a civilian pilot's license, I would be a shoo-in for military flight training. This was a good move, because we could do flight training at nearby Rickenbacker Field, which was named for Eddie Rickenbacker, the World War I ace and Medal of Honor recipient. I would get to know him well later in life.

By the way, I hate it when people say "Medal of Honor winner." It is not a prize, not a contest. It is our nation's highest award to recognize a man for his service to the nation. And do not misunderstand me. In no way do I feel that I deserved that medal for being a pilot. There is a little guilt in wearing it, because there were so many men far braver than I, and who even died serving our nation. I think about that all the time. I was just lucky, so I try and represent the Marine Corps and the Air National Guard, as well as the medal, with reverence. It is a sacred trust, really. My roommate, Fred Smith, joined the Marine Corps. He sent letters telling me about training, and I knew it was tough. The Marines is not for everyone. When I saw him in the dress blue uniform, that was my final hook. Somehow, someway, I was going to be a Marine Corps pilot. That was my primary objective. Then I went on a hitchhiking escapade with my buddy Ralph [Gunvordahl] on our way to Minneapolis to enlist in the Marines. Ralph knew Boyington, Tex Hill, Dick Rossi, Chuck Older, and those guys because he later flew with the Flying Tigers. More about him later. He was a great guy, and he disliked Boyington just like most of the men did.

Well, Europe was on fire because Hitler had invaded Poland. Britain and France declared war on Germany. Then Hitler invaded every country in western Europe except Britain. The speed of the German conquests was staggering, with the last major prize, France, falling in about a month. It was unbelievable to us. After I graduated from the university, I reported to Wold-Chamberlain Base in Minneapolis [U.S. Naval Air Station (NAS) Minneapolis] for ground school. America was rapidly rebuilding the military, which had basically been allowed to fall apart after the First World War.

Aviation recruiters were all over the place doing interviews and giving aptitude tests. This was the rationale for the E flight program—"E" for elimination. It was a five-week process. They wanted to weed out early anyone who would have wasted time and money later down the road. The course was pretty rigorous. We studied navigation in all its forms, meteorology, and Morse code. If you passed all these tests, you started to learn to fly. I already had the basic principles down to a science due to my flying experience.

During downtime I kept up with the news. The newspapers were full of stories about what was happening in Europe. Japan had taken French Indochina, which we called Vietnam two decades later. The Selective Service Act was started, and men were required to sign up to enter the military as draftees if they did not voluntarily enlist. I had a girlfriend named June Shakstad, and she was cool about the military. I guess back in those days it was considered a high honor to serve in uniform despite the relatively low pay.

My class had twelve guys who survived the initial selection and two others who were Marine options. The rest were Navy guys. Our primary instructor was a Marine captain named Avery Kier, the kind of Marine I wanted to be. He was just a class act all the way around. I had never divulged my hundred or so hours of logged flight time. I did not want to draw any attention or be graded at a level above the others. I wanted to be treated fairly and on equal terms. Also, sometimes you got an instructor who might be personally offended if he had a trainee with a lot of experience. Attitudes and bad blood could get you tossed out, too. The other problem was the fear that they would take my prior experience and make me an instructor pilot. That was not what I wanted.

That course was a cakewalk for me. The nine of us who graduated received orders to the Naval Air Station at Pensacola,

Florida, for seven months. I also had a month of earned leave, so I went back home and helped out the family. When I arrived at Pensacola, I felt I was in heaven. We had the basic aviation and aeronautical training, but we also had a lot of physical conditioning, and I was very good at it because I was in great shape. Our PT [physical training] instructor was boxing champion Gene Tunney. He beat Jack Dempsey for the title, and we were in awe of him. Part of our training included boxing and I did OK. We got in better shape with sports and a lot of running and push-ups, sit-ups, things like that. I spent six months there and loved every minute of it.

Part of this story you will enjoy. One of my flight instructors in Pensacola was Greg Boyington. This was when I first met him, before his AVG [Flying Tiger] days. He was a gambler, as was I, and we played poker quite often. Once, after I lost thirty bucks to him, we went to craps, and I won that back and more. Boyington was a different kind of character even back then, and it never crossed my mind that we would meet again during the war. I have to admit that he was a very detail-oriented and thoughtful instructor.

I was transferred to Miami to learn to fly fighters at Opa-locka Naval Air Station, where we trained on that F4B4 that I had seen back home. This was intensive flying, all the twists, rolls, climbs, and dives needed to know how to survive intense combat. When I later arrived at my operational unit, that training became invaluable. Learning your limitations with g-forces and negative g-forces was also critical. Even though your instruments such as the altimeter, artificial horizon, and the turn-bank indicator would guide you in these maneuvers, it was good to be self-aware of your attitude and angles. I was really good at all of that whichever position I was in. Aerobatics washed a lot of guys out in mock dogfights. Some guys could not get the hang of a hard banking turn and roll, and we were graded on all of it.

After that phase came aerial gunnery training. This was what I was waiting for. Some of us were picked for a medical evaluation to determine the effects of flying on pilots. Later this became an ongoing process to determine if there were adverse side effects on pilots and to assess their continued fitness to fly. This was where a lot of guys were dropped as fighter pilots. Some went to dive-bombers or torpedo bombers as a result of not being able to hit towed targets. Their greatest problem was not giving lead on the moving target. It came down to basic geometry and trigonometry. I was not a math major. I just had good experience shooting critters on the run, adjusting for high wind and leading targets.

On March 15, 1941, I received my commission as a second lieutenant, and on March 29, 1941, I received my wings. I was called into the CO's office and handed my orders. I rapidly read them, and my heart hit the floor. I was being assigned as a primary flight instructor [IP]. That was almost as bad as a desk job. I really wanted to be in a unit that would see action when the time came. I knew that IPs often spent their entire career stateside training pilots and never got overseas. Now, do not get me wrong. I respected good instructors, and God knows we needed them, but that was just not my idea of a fighter pilot. I always thought that the married men should be chosen first as IPs and let us single guys get to the frontline units.

I asked why and was told that I was somewhat older than the other pilots, and they wanted young guys with fast reflexes and more time left on their biological clock ready to fight. I would train them. I packed my bags as my classmates whooped and hollered when they saw their assignments to fighter squadrons. I felt like the odd man out. So I went to Saufley Field, which still kept me in Pensacola.

The only good thing about being a primary flight instructor was the flying time. I logged a butt load of hours, sometimes six hours a day, teaching new guys the basics. We flew the N3N trainer. It also allowed me to experiment with new maneuvers, things I just thought up, so that part was quite fun. I had to sort out those guys who had the head for flying and those who did not. It was usually pretty easy. But being a training pilot also had its problems, because there was always the stress of having a young pilot who might panic or make some bonehead blunder, and then I had to take control.

All the hours were exhausting—flying, paperwork, inspections, you name it. Sometimes you have moments where you really wish you could start the day over. One of these happened when I was with a student pilot doing maneuvers on command. We were at four hundred feet when I told him to cut the engine. He did a snap roll instead and inverted us, but my arms were pinned by the g-force, and by the time I was able to reach the controls, we crashed. Well, we survived with bruises on both bodies and egos. That guy was gone.

What I hated was the paperwork. Administrative duties were the bane of a fighter pilot. The more rank I got, the more paperwork came with it. When you had a crash—let alone an injury or, God help, a fatality—the paperwork hit like an avalanche. We did lose instructors and student pilots. It happens because flying is a dangerous business. I did that job for nine months and I hated it, but I had to accept the fact that the many hours of flying, the experience of unpredictability, with unknowns from mechanical problems to panicked students, prepared me for a lot of what I would experience later.

I was off on Sunday, December 7, 1941, and I always took my time off seriously. I would fish or hunt at the Everglades and beaches, bag some game or fish, and we would eat them at the officers' mess. That morning I went shooting doves with another Marine and two Navy pilots. I had to get back to assume my duties, but we stopped to trade the birds at a small restaurant we knew for a meal. We stepped in and it was like entering a different world. Everyone seemed very serious, and a few were listening to the radio, playing the music of the day. That was when we were told about Pearl Harbor. We dropped the birds and headed straight back to base. The ride was not the usual casual banter. We were pretty silent, all in our own thoughts. We knew it was war. I am sure the other guys were thinking what I was thinking. Where will they send me, if anywhere? Without a radio in the truck the drive was a silent torture.

We got back and I ran to get into uniform when the CO stopped me. He said I was in charge, double the guard at all access points. I also had to locate all the men and get them back as soon as possible. Since it was a Sunday, they were scattered to the winds, but a few came back. I ordered them to go and find the others. Get on phones, call girlfriends, scour the bars, but get them back. Then I was ordered to triple the guard, but there were still not enough men to comply with the first order. I did place armed men on the airfield to guard the planes, the armory, and fuel depot in case of any sabotage attempts.

One funny part of this story was that I had to check the sentries guarding the long line of aircraft. We had over a hundred trainers all lined up. The men were armed as expected. I was riding a bicycle to check on the men when one of them heard me coming and yelled "Halt!" He was nervous as hell and pointing that Thompson submachine gun at me. That forced me to stop very quickly in the loose gravel, and I fell off, tearing the cuff of my trousers and cutting my hand. I was quite pissed off.

I calmed down and realized that he was doing his job correctly. The next day we learned exactly what had happened at Pearl Harbor, the number of ships and aircraft destroyed and the casualties, over three thousand. I felt sick to my stomach, but I knew that we were now in a world war. We declared war on Japan, and then Germany and Italy, as allies of Japan declared war on us. The stupid part about that was that neither Italy nor

Germany was bound by any treaty to declare war in support of Japan. Hitler and Mussolini just thought it was a good idea. That would prove to be a bad decision.

Well, I knew that I had to get into the shooting war. There was no way in hell I was going to be left out of the biggest show in history. I applied for a transfer to a combat unit, but it was again denied due to my age. Then I figured out there might be another way. If I could volunteer for any assignment, even if not a combat job, that would get me to another command. I might get a more sympathetic response to my desire to fly combat. I applied for glider training but was placed on a waiting list.

Finally, by applying for all the crazy things that came up, I was sent to photography school, which was still in Pensacola. I found it laborious and boring, but I learned everything about photography and film, including developing, printing, cutting, splicing, framing, you name it. I passed the course and was assigned to VMD-1, the first photographic reconnaissance unit in the Marine Corps, which got me to San Diego. Ironically, my girlfriend from Sioux Falls, June, was out there as well working in La Jolla. I thought that this might just work out all the way around.

June was a smart girl who graduated from Iowa State University. She knew that most Marines, especially pilots, ended up in California, and in San Diego for the most part. So she took a job out there, expecting me to arrive at some point. She was right. Here I was, but I wanted out of that photo-recon job and a transfer to a real combat unit. We had several aircraft for photographic-reconnaissance-training purposes, some SNJ Texan trainers, with which we were all familiar. One thing I found out was that there was not a lot of flying to be done and that was kind of disappointing. To add to my continued misery, I could see the pilots on the other side of the base flying the Grumman F4F Wildcats, which was what I wanted to do. Whenever I saw those planes, I felt a little more depressed.

When I hit the ground and got settled in, I went to the base commander, Colonel [Al] Cooley, and requested a transfer. Once again, I was told that I was too old to be a combat fighter pilot. I was getting really tired of hearing that. I was now the junior officer in the unit, which meant few major responsibilities, and I could spend time with June since she lived and worked nearby. That sort of eased the pain of being in pilot purgatory. But my mind was always working out the problem. I was not going to be sidelined in the world war, no way in hell.

But then my fortunes changed for the better, because the squadron CO, [Lieutenant Colonel] Ed Pollack, selected me to fly as his wingman on business trips and such. This was a great gig indeed. We would fly the trainer to wherever he had to go, drop him off, and I would fly it back. That was great for me because I was able to log more hours and keep current in my flight log. I discussed my plight with him and he was very sympathetic to my situation. We actually became good friends despite the disparity in rank. He knew I was a very competent pilot. He also knew that men like me, contrary to conventional wisdom, would be needed in the war.

There was another bright light. It was determined that the photo-recon pilots needed to be trained in fighter tactics in order to evade enemy fighters that would probably have a real interest in bagging one of them, so I volunteered immediately for the training. This would increase my flight time and my profile among the powers that be. I figured that there was no downside. That was until I was told that the Navy did not want any Marines. Then the depression set in again, but I was far from being done. Cooley gave me permission to go over and talk with them. I was told that if they accepted me, I would have orders cut for the transfer.

Well, I went over and reported to the Navy CO [Commander Jessie Young]. He was not interested in me at all, even after he knew that I had trained Navy pilots in Pensacola. I was "too old, and a Marine. That is it." Well, that was what he said. I knew that there was always another entrance if the door was locked. I then learned that they were detaching men for funeral details, including notification parties, escorts, and funeral ceremony duty. No one liked that duty. It struck close to home, whether it was a death in training or a man brought back from overseas. Pilots are a superstitious group. I knew guys who would always wear the same pair of socks on missions or would lace their shoes a certain way—crazy things to civilians and nonaviators. I knew one guy in the Pacific who would not fly unless the chaplain blessed his crucifix and threw holy water on it.

Once I learned about the problems of getting volunteers for the funeral details, I went back to the CO [Young]. I told him I would do anything to be a part of the program—clean the hangars, even funeral duties. That made him realize I was very determined, because no one volunteered for funeral detail. That was the morale-killing equivalent of a gear-up landing. No one wanted to be a part of it. Well, that got me in with a probationary period. If I did not screw up, then I was good to go. This half-assed barter system then allowed me to start flying the F4F [Wildcat] with the Navy lieutenant [Ed Pawka]. I loved the Wildcat, compared to all the other planes I flew up to that time.

If you factor in our weapons, six fifties against the Jap seven-millimeter machine guns and the twenty-millimeter cannon, there was no real contest. In addition, I mention the self-sealing tanks and armor plate. That really increased our survivability, whereas the Zero had none of that. They [the Japanese] sacrificed the added weight of pilot protection for speed, maneuverability, and range, and they paid for it. In fact, over Guadalcanal and throughout the Solomon Islands alone, the Japs lost at least six to seven hundred aircraft and Wildcats took out most of them.

Even worse than losing the planes, losing all those experienced fighter pilots, some with years of combat experience, really kicked them in the balls. From what I understand, by 1943 they were never able to train enough skilled pilots to replace the ones we had knocked out. By 1944, they were having to throw kids with minimal training into the cockpits, mostly for kamikaze missions.

Well, getting back to the training unit, it really was pretty good duty, and I got to log a lot of hours. When we got the Wildcats, we all had to qualify for carrier takeoff and landing. They had this wooden-decked mock-up out on the runway. It was just like an aircraft carrier deck, marked up and with a trap wire. The Wildcat had a retractable tail wheel and tailhook to catch the cable on a carrier. I got really good at it, and it only made you a better pilot, especially when you had to control speed, flaps and use that artificial horizon and altimeter. This became critical in limited visibility.

Another thing I was very good at was aerial gunnery. As I said before, I grew up shooting critters on the run, pulling lead, all of that. Hitting a target sleeve towed by another aircraft was easy as hell in comparison. This sleeve was about the size of a Wildcat in length, and it was attached by a three-hundred-foot cable. This added to the safety of the towing pilot. Each pilot had different-colored bullets so that the instructors could see who was on target and who was missing it completely. We would practice a high-angle deflection attack, climbing and then peeling from above, and roll over to engage the target sleeve.

Flying that damned towplane was a duty I was willing to accept. I loved logging the hours. There were in fact a few accidents where the towplane was shot up. I would rather be tied to a beehive smeared in honey than be the student pilot who shot down a towplane, let alone killed the pilot. I knew that I had to return to the photo-recon unit at some point, but I was working out a way to avoid that. When I paid them a visit, they still had not received any new aircraft.

Then a small miracle happened. I stepped into the CO's

office [Colonel Parmly] and he told me that I was being transferred to Camp Kearny, which is near San Diego. I was to take
over as the new executive officer of VMF-121. Since we were at
war, I knew that would mean a deployment overseas, and I was
all geared up for it. I replaced the previous first lieutenant, who
became the operations officer. When I arrived, I met the forty
pilots who were not too happy with getting a new XO [execu-
tive officer], since they liked the man I had replaced. Well, I
took the time to get to know them, and over time I eventually
had a great working relationship with them.

I met our CO, Major Leonard Davis. His nickname was
"Duke." He was a Naval Academy graduate and professional career Marine pilot, but to look at him, you would have never assumed any of that. He was a skinny guy, energetic, intelligent
with a good sense of humor. Soon we all had nicknames. Because I smoked cigars, I was Smokey Joe, and you know how
that goes. I think nicknames are a universal constant in all air
forces. I met a lot of German pilots over the years, and even
they had nicknames during the war. Later on, military nicknames would become call signs.

We did not get to fly together very much because we were
preparing for deployment. I had no real idea how these men
flew as a unit. We knew that we were getting into the war. Of
course, then I had to have a discussion with my new wife [June].
We also heard that on August 2 [1942] the 1st Marine Division
had landed at Guadalcanal, the southernmost island in the Solomon Islands. They took the Japanese airfield, which was named

for one of the great pilots who fought at Wake Island during the Japanese invasion [Henderson Field].

The Marines hit that island and fought like hell, but their only air support was from carriers for a while because the airfield was not completed. The Seabees came in to complete the strip, and once it was set up, we would go in and join the one VMF already staging there for air operations. I felt sorry for those mud Marines. Even though they held the airfield and some surrounding jungle, the Japs still controlled the rest of the island, and they wanted to take that airfield back badly. We heard about the casualties as the Japs relentlessly attacked the Marines to get that airfield back. We heard about Chesty Puller and his men doing impossible things. We had a lot to talk about with the downtime waiting to ship out, and pilots hate downtime.

On September 1, 1942, we boarded a ship named the *Matsonia* and moved out to the South Pacific. Our Wildcats were shipped on a carrier [the escort carrier *Copahee*]. We knew this was going to get hot as soon as we arrived, and we all looked forward to it. The S-2 briefings were steady and, as I found out, pretty inaccurate regarding the air battles around the Solomons, and especially regarding enemy aircraft strengths and capabilities. We would learn about all of that firsthand after we arrived in Guadalcanal.

Well, seasickness took a toll on a few guys, but we all survived. Our quarters were cramped as hell and hot as hell, too. It was more like a sauna with eight of us officers packed in like sardines. At night all the portholes were closed and locked, so no light would be seen from outside. There was a real fear of Jap subs patrolling the area, especially as we neared the Solomon chain.

The most mind-numbing thing about being on a ship like this was the boredom. To break that up, we played games, and poker games broke out all over the ship. I was always a pretty good poker player and I ended up winning over $2,000 when it was all over. Well, of course that money went back home to June because what was I going to do with it?

We did a lot to occupy our time. We had classes on everything from first aid, navigation refreshers, and tactics. We were well indoctrinated in the Thach Weave tactic also. This was a tactic devised by [Navy Lieutenant Commander, later Rear Admiral] John [Smith] Thach. It was developed to counter the more maneuverable Zeros in a dogfight, giving our pilots a chance at engaging on more equal terms. We all knew about Butch O'Hare and the others who used it with great effect.

We learned that a flight of sixteen fighters flying in two elements was a great formation even against superior numbers of enemies. If everyone was on the same page, we would have great success.

At the end of September [1942], we docked in New Caledonia, where our fighters also arrived on that carrier. We changed ships and prepared to launch the Wildcats off and land at our new air base [Tontouta]. When the planes were transported, the wings were always folded to save space on the deck, so we had to unfold and lock them into place. Crew chiefs did the last checks, and then we were told to mount up. The CO would launch first, and I would follow last. This was just procedure to ensure that all the pilots got off all right. This was my first catapult launch, so I was a little nervous, but excited when they turned the ship into the light wind. This was done to provide the most lift possible.

After many hours of practicing landing on a carrier mock-up on an airfield, this was a totally new experience, mainly because of the slow roll of the carrier on the ocean, not just the catapult experience. Revving up that engine, feeling the power, watching my gauges, I also had to look over at the launch officer. When the time was right, I had to release the brake and then the catapult cable thrust the Wildcat forward and pushed me back into the seat. Once airborne, I looked out over the ocean and the island itself.

We all landed safely despite the heavy crosswind. I mean it was a strong one. One pilot [Bill Freeman] dipped a wing and cartwheeled, which we call a ground loop, but he came out of it unhurt. Those were usually fatal even under the best of circumstances. There was no wind sock, nothing but the flag on a flagpole or the palm trees to show you the wind direction and allow you to compensate. We did not even have a tower controller giving us wind speed and direction; we just had to deal with it. Well, that pilot spent the next few weeks getting his fighter put back together, using whatever spare parts he and the ground crew could find. That kind of thing happens on occasion. Even the CO, Duke, had a touch-and-go, bouncing on one wheel to apply rudder to correct for this crosswind, so there was no punishment.

While we waited for our orders to relocate to Guadalcanal, we continued receiving after-action reports from other pilots, some dating back to June during Midway. We studied these, and all had some degree of skepticism regarding the abilities of the Zero. But there were a couple of pilots who had fought against them on New Caledonia, and we took their advice above anything S-2 gave us. We learned about the speed, agility, and climbing ability, and, even more important, their turning radius in a dogfight. I mentally catalogued all of this information. I knew that our Thach Weave was a good tactic.

On October 6 we received our orders and flew to the carrier USS *Long Island* and after landing took some rest. We were headed toward the Solomons, Guadalcanal, and our new home base. We all openly talked about our pending combat. Sure, you had some nervousness, but despite the Japs having more combat experience, we all firmly believed that with our training and Wildcats we would be the better side. We could also operate at a higher altitude than other fighters at that time. Not even the P-40 could reach our ceiling, as we had the two-stage superchargers.

On the third day of nothing but downtime, we were told to pack our bags and load up. We expected about two to three more days on the ship, but reports came back that Japanese submarines were patrolling the area, and it was thought best just to launch us once we were within range to protect the ship and the aircraft. I was happy to get the news, to be honest. We took off from the carrier and formed up, then headed to Guadalcanal. After just over three hours, we saw it ahead. I thought it looked great—beautiful light blue-green sea and dark blue ocean, just green all over the place because of the jungle.

We had a great group of guys flying there, such as Marion Carl, Bill Freeman, Frank Presley, Roger Haberman, and Greg Loesch, who often flew as my main wingman. We had a nickname, the "Flying Circus." We were quite a group, I can tell you. Morale was always high. We looked forward to mixing it up with the Zekes. I think every fighter pilot has that hunter-killer instinct, that desire to prove himself, like all warriors, and definitely all Marines, do.

As we closed in on Henderson Field, we saw the airstrip that had just been carved out of the jungle and scraped flat by bulldozers. I could easily see all of the holes in the ground from the Japanese bombers that were always pounding the base, breaking the Marston Matting. After each attack the Seabees filled the holes and leveled it out again. Otherwise, landing anything would have been impossible. Upon landing, we were directed to the parking area, where the packed dirt was covered with steel plates. This was to prevent the fighters from sinking into the mud during heavy rain, and it rained a lot.

I had not even unstrapped when a bunch of guys came out

of the jungle, unwashed, unshaved clowns. These were the ground crews for the torpedo and dive-bombers and antiaircraft gunners. They were happy as hell to see us and help us out. Without adequate fighter cover, they just had to sit there and take the poundings that the Japs gave them, with little recourse. I remember this one guy walked up and offered me a coconut with the top cut off.

"Here you go, sir. Have a drink. Welcome to hell!"

Well, I drank it, my first taste of coconut milk, and I liked it. I liked eating them also, but after a few weeks, they got to be a little old. These guys had been through a lot and you could see it. Then we looked over and saw the edge of the airfield, and there were a lot of damaged planes, shot up and just wrecks. We learned that most had been damaged in the bombing raids, others shot up flying missions. Then we had another surprise. A jeep pulled up and we met Major John Smith. He readily informed us that we had landed on the bomber airstrip; ours was just under a mile away. We found that out when the new dive-bomber unit arrived on the airstrip, commanded by my old instrument flight instructor, Eddie Miller, from Pensacola. Smith said, "Welcome to Cactus," the call sign for Guadalcanal. That was how we got the nickname the Cactus Air Force. [*Smith would be credited with nineteen victories after two months on Guadalcanal.*]

We also met the guys of VMF-223, who had been there almost two months flying the only fighter operations. Their stories were interesting as well as sobering. They got shelled from Jap ships, hit by bombers. They were flying daily, always outnumbered. There were almost no spare parts, no replacement aircraft, and just getting engine oil, ammunition, and gasoline supplies were major endeavors. They also told us to expect to be wet and hot all the time, especially now that we were in the rainy season, which would last well into March. I also ran into an old friend from San Diego, First Lieutenant Ben Finney. He was a guy with the best stories from his years in the Hollywood crowd. He was discharged with a Purple Heart from World War I, and he was an officer and a great guy. I think he was the oldest lieutenant in the entire Marine Corps but am not sure. He was in his mid-forties.

I took it all in. I was amazed at the amount of wildlife we saw. Lovely colored birds were everywhere, the largest butterflies and spiders I have ever seen, big-ass crocodiles on the banks of the Lunga River, where we were supposed to take baths, and even bigger-ass crocs swimming in the ocean, which was also filled with sharks. Then there were the mosquitoes. They were not so bad near the airstrip when there was a good wind, but when you went into the jungle or inside a tent, those ravenous little bastards would feed on you. I say little, but they were actually quite large. You could hear them, too, coming in a swarm sounding like small Pratt and Whitney engines. We were all swelling up from bites and issued quinine damned near daily to fend off malaria. They would land on you by the dozens, and when you wiped them off, your hand would be black and often bloody. Those bastards ate well.

I also learned that the men were always low on rations. They had to go hunt shit and kill it to eat sometimes. Some of the locals had a few cows, and the Marines and Army guys put their money together to buy one every now and then, but most of the locals had no need for hard currency. They pretty much lived on the barter system. There was a big problem that we learned about our supply ships: they would not deliver much-needed matériel to us. That pissed me off. Then we learned that there was also this crazy infighting within the military. Some senior flag officers wanted to reinforce Guadalcanal as a staging platform to continue the island-hopping campaign. Others wanted to bypass it and leave it to the Japs, because they considered the place a wasted effort. While they bitched and bickered, the soldiers, sailors, and Marines suffered for lack of almost everything we needed.

The Marine pilots who had been there awhile welcomed us. They saw us as a group to relieve some of the pressure. I became best friends with Marion Carl, who was a captain then, and also Major Robert Galer. Those two along with Major Smith would be credited with forty-six enemy fighters destroyed, earning them the nickname the "Three Flying Fools of Guadalcanal." Of the three, Marion was the guy I immediately liked. Marion and I were the best of friends up until he was murdered by that prick.

[*I interviewed Major General Marion Carl several times by telephone in 1989 and 1996. His first combat was at Midway, and he scored a victory. Over Henderson Field he killed Japanese ace Junichi Sasai on August 26, 1942. Carl was the first ace in the United States Marine Corps and ended the war with 18.5 victories, ranked seventh among Marine Corps aces. Carl later learned to fly jets, was a test pilot, and commanded VMF-122, the first Marine jet squadron. He also learned to fly helicopters and flew missions in both types in Vietnam. His book,* Pushing the Envelope, *written with Barrett Tillman, is highly suggested reading. Marion Carl was killed with a shotgun by a home intruder who also wounded his wife, Edna. His murderer, nineteen-year-old Jesse Fanus, was apprehended one week later. He received the death penalty, which was later overturned, and a life sentence without parole was adjudicated. During his career Marion Carl earned two Navy Crosses, among other awards. He was a great man.]*

Even though we were well established at Henderson Field, there was still fighting raging in the hills. We could hear the mortar and machine-gun fire, sporadic rifle shots. We had the occasional mortar round land in the perimeter. Then we had this fool we called "Maytag Charlie," who flew over at night, dropping grenades or just garbage on the field. We still had the occasional Jap sniper in the hills taking shots at people. One day I was with the ground crew, who were repairing my Wildcat, when a rifle shot was heard, and a sharp zing went by. Some damned Jap was nearby shooting at us. Well, this young guy—a ground crewman, I think—said he had "had enough of this shit" and grabbed his pistol and headed off into the jungle. Not long afterward we heard another shot. Sometime later this guy came walking out with a Jap rifle. He found the sniper in a tree and took him out.

On another occasion we had one of those nocturnal bomber raids, but this was a lone Betty [twin-engine level bomber], I guess, who just wanted to harass us. I guess the entire ground contingent had had just about enough of that horseshit and every man, pilot to mechanic, came out with pistols, rifles, and machine guns when the bomber came in low to strafe after dropping its payload. They fired up at it, leading the target. I know they must have hit the damned thing, but it did not catch fire or crash. Against the dark sky, that would have been spectacular. My fighter had minor damage other than the joystick being shot away.

Once when we were getting shelled, I dove into a preexisting shell hole, and these other Marines jumped into another one. A shell landed in their hole and killed them. I thought right then and there how lucky I was to choose that hole. Makes you think, you know? Once I jumped into a shell hole only to find that it was a small swimming pool.

Our first mission was as an escort for dive-bombers, so our eight Wildcats flew top cover. We never had any contact with enemy fighters, but the bombers hit a Jap destroyer, so that mission was a good one. We had an alert the next day [October 11, 1942] that we had incoming aircraft. Sure enough, twenty-eight bombers and twenty-one Zeros were coming in. Their bombers dropped their ordnance far short of our guys, and a couple of the enemy planes were shot down, but I never even got close to the battle.

But that day was not over by a long shot. That night there was a naval battle. The Japs lost around six ships and we lost a destroyer, but the Japs still managed to land a few thousand of their soldiers on the island as reinforcements. There was no doubt that their objective was to retake the airfield. We saw the debris of the battle on the beach the next morning. We were up in the air at dawn, escorting the dive-bombers. They were to engage any enemy ships still in the area. They were headed up the slot, as we called it, and we saw two destroyers off the coast of New Georgia. Our fighters went in as a diversion, and the bombers hit a destroyer and sank a cruiser, and we had no losses.

The next day [October 12], we scrambled for an intercept but never made contact. Then a couple of hours later we had another alert. We were in the air and soon caught sight of them—eighteen medium bombers with an escort of six Zeros. We had altitude advantage at twenty-two thousand feet. I saw the Zeros and looked over at my wingman, Greg Loesch. He was waving like a madman, and I nodded to let him know I saw the Zeros, when he peeled away. Suddenly I could not see anyone from my flight, but I did see the tracers fly past my canopy from ahead and below. That was when I knew my radio was not working. He had tried to warn me. But I was a firm believer that good communications made for a better fighting unit.

Well, having no communications almost cost me my life. I saw the Zero pass and I pulled up, as did the Jap. He passed to within a hundred yards of my guns and I was closing, as he was in a slight turn due to his maneuverability. I led him slightly, fired, and he went smoking and on fire into the sea. However, in my excitement I failed to see the three Zeros coming in on me, and after the first few tracers went by my canopy, I threw the stick forward and went into a power dive. Well, my airspeed indicator was reading over four hundred and I still had these bastards on my tail. Right then and there, I thought that the intelligence on our superiority in a dive was bullshit propaganda.

I felt more rounds hit my plane and saw oil streaming out from the right cooler, and my engine temperature rose rapidly. Then I was covered by smoke with bright flashes of tracer rounds peppering my fuselage. I really thought that I had screwed up and was dead. My canopy was shattered, I had a large hole in my right wing that allowed me to see the blue ocean underneath me, the propeller was windmilling uncontrollably, and my engine was dead. I went into an even steeper dive, and the air pressure was incredible. The excess drag of the damaged prop increased the vibrations, so I pulled up a bit to relieve the vibrations. I was afraid the Wildcat was going to break up.

I pulled back on the stick and was at about 150 feet above the deck, just skimming over the trees and headed for the airfield. My airspeed indicator still worked, and I was doing about 150 knots. I was coming in way too fast to land, but I knew that if I bled off airspeed, the Zeros following me would catch up and finish me off. The only way to slow down was to lower the landing gear because my flaps did not work. I managed to crunch down and roll through some trees. Luckily the antiaircraft gunners dissuaded my pursuers and they broke off. I sat there in that smoking cockpit, amazed that I was alive, not even wounded. That was when I heard the ambulance coming.

I felt bad. Sure, I bagged a kill, but I also lost my own fighter in the process. I climbed out, feeling like an idiot, but when the rest of the guys landed, they were all congratulating me. That made me feel a lot better. I learned a few major lessons on that flight. I would never be unaware of my surroundings, and I would never rely on the radio to be my early-warning system. If you do not have communications, you are at a great disadvantage, so see everything. I confirmed a kill for Bill Freeman, who managed a bomber kill when he dove into a group of them.

Not long afterward we had a night attack. We were in our tents when the Japs dropped parachute flares for illumination. Then it all happened. We were bombed from the air for a while, and two hours of large-caliber naval shells landed all over the airfield. We lost a fuel dump and the ammo dump. The sky was as bright as day, tracers and showers of light all over the night sky. Shrapnel pierced everything. Here we were in our fighting holes, helpless. We fared better than the dive-bomber pilots. They never prepared foxholes for cover, and they were hit by all that shrapnel. I think around a dozen of those guys were killed and many were wounded.

Most of the aircraft were heavily damaged and many destroyed. I don't think there was a single bird that did not have extensive damage. The ground crews got to work right away with repairs. Then we had the problem of losing our fuel. All the preparations that old Ben Finney had made us do had paid off. [*Finney had Foss and his men dig deep foxholes, with sand-bagged walls and camouflage tents to enhance protection from attack.*] He then had another bright idea. He thought that the Japs might have had spotters in the hills, or perhaps a Jap recon plane might fly overhead and report on how successful they had been in destroying our fighting capability. He had us rig together mock-ups of fighters from scrap metal, cardboard, anything to resemble fighters at the end of the airfield. This would hopefully make the enemy think that we were still a viable fighting force. Otherwise, they would most probably come back in strength, knowing that we could not mount a defense.

Then, as if that was not bad enough, we had not even cleared all the debris when the air-raid siren went off. We only had seven fighters available. The guys had just lifted off and their gear was still down when the first wave of Zeros came in to attack. Our seven Wildcats managed to survive that attack and climb, but the Zeros left quickly; it was just a hit-and-run. Meanwhile, our metal workers and mechanics were still scrounging and cannibalizing aircraft for spare parts. Hell, they even culled through crashed Jap aircraft for anything they could use. They worked night and day to patch up what would fly and strip parts from what would never fly, just to keep us operational.

During downtime we listened to the radio. We could get Armed Forces Network and Tokyo Rose, an American woman working for the Japanese. Her propaganda broadcasts were meant to demoralize us, with shit like "Your wives are sleeping with those men back home while you do the hard fighting," and that kind of crap. I enjoyed listening to her, as did the other guys. [*Iva Ikuko Toguri D'Aquino was an American citizen charged with treason after the war. She was pardoned by President Gerald R. Ford.*]

I think it was the next day when we were scrambled to intercept a flight of Betty bombers. My plane was fixed, so we took off. In just a few minutes, we saw a large formation of bombers and a bunch of Zero escort fighters. Then my engine began to sputter. Three times it coughed, started, and then sputtered. I told Loesch to take over. I had engine problems. I was pissed off as hell, I can tell you. I had to hide in a cloud bank until the Japs finished hitting my airfield.

But then I saw a Wildcat swoop down with a Zero square on his ass, and they did not see me, despite being less than thirty feet away and almost colliding with me. I just applied a little right rudder, and from a range of about fifty yards or less, I pulled the trigger. Easy kill. Well, as I came in to land, I saw my kill still burning on the hillside. I got out and stomped over to the maintenance shack. I was pissed off like you would not believe. But after they checked, they confirmed that it was not a mechanical issue. The fuel was dirty, and it fouled the fuel system and carburetor. Others had similar problems.

After the disastrous raid, we set up a large ground fuel holding tank, and every drop of gas we took from the tanks of all the damaged aircraft that would not fly, even cans we had delivered, were poured into it. It was hidden in the jungle with palm and coconut trees and a camouflage net to try and hide it from the air. Our base commander sent out a request for fuel. That request went all the way to General [Alexander] Vandegrift, who requested all fuel available be delivered to us. General [Roy] Geiger, a Marine pilot in command of an infantry division, supported that request. The reports from the Navy said a major Jap naval force was steaming toward us again, part of what we called the "Tokyo Express."

Troop transports and supply ships, thousands of enemy soldiers were coming, and we were powerless to stop them with air support for the ground troops. We received a visit from Colonel Toby Munn. Geiger had sent him to tell us that the last of the fuel would be used to attack the convoy; then we would join the infantry to hold off the invasion. I can tell you, right then and there, pilot morale dropped lower than a snake's balls.

Well, the SBD dive-bombers took off and I was leading their fighter escort. You have to understand that these dive-bombers flew slow as hell, and they were carrying these one-thousand-pound bombs, real monsters. Just one could sink the largest Jap ship if it hit in the right spot. We saw six transports in a single file with destroyer escorts, just north on Guadalcanal. They were running up the slot big-time. We fighters dropped down to get their attention by strafing, one at a time. The gunners were throwing up shells at both us and the dive-bombers, and we flew up from behind and just fired into the soldiers in the open transports. The dive-bombers sank one transport but then the attack broke off.

During this attack I lost Lieutenant Paul Rutledge, who was shot down and crashed among the troopships. Another pilot was wounded but able to fly. Another pilot named Andy Andrews did the craziest thing I ever saw. He peeled over and went back, all alone, and began strafing the troopships head-on, then weaving so that the gunners on both destroyers and transports would risk hitting their own ships firing at him. The tracers were all around him, and he was rolling, slipping, diving, and climbing and rolling again, then turning for another run.

Now, this was really nuts and he made six passes, hitting those transports. I still chewed his ass out when he landed, just as the next flight led by our CO took off to continue the attack on the same convoy. We had word that we lost another pilot and the flight had to break contact due to the heavy volume of fire. We all knew that now, being out of fuel, we were doomed. There was nothing more we could do.

I sat in my foxhole, waiting for the inevitable shells to hit the field again, or bombers to drop their loads on top of us. I kept a diary, and I wrote in it that the "shit is about to hit the fan." At 0200 we were hit by over seven hundred shells from the Jap ships. They targeted the fighter strip, where all the remaining fighters were located. We found out that the Japs had also dropped four thousand more soldiers on the beach just ten miles away from us. They had tanks, artillery, and a lot of motivation. We didn't have shit. We were low on ammo and had no fuel even to fly air operations to support the Seventh Marines holding the line. But the Japs actually launched attacks to re-take the airfield, and Chesty Puller's group broke it off in their ass and killed around three thousand Japs in a couple of large attacks. Vandegrift commanded the Marine and Army ground forces, and I believe that was where John Basilone earned his Medal of Honor in October.

Well, when the airfields were finished, we had everyone there, Army, Navy, Marines, and all the aircraft from fighters, me-dium bombers, dive-bombers, and torpedo bombers. And here is a great story. A search ordered by General Geiger, based solely on a rumor, sparked a treasure hunt, and the effort found over four hundred gallons of gasoline buried in caches that had been placed there a couple of months earlier. We were just never in-formed about it. However, and this is the craziest part of the story, Geiger had a letter in his pocket that he had not opened in a long time. When he did open it, it was instructions on where the emergency fuel was stored. So we went through many days of no fuel, then to scrounging for fuel, just to find fuel. And that could have been done much sooner.

We immediately began straining and pouring fuel into the Wildcats when we heard there were Zeros overhead. I looked up and saw five Japs, up high. But they did not attack, strafe, or anything. Then they peeled away. Then we heard that Jap bombers were on the way. Then it hit me. They had just marked a target indicator in the sky for the bombers to get a fix on the ground targets. Smart, I thought.

Well, we scrambled fourteen fighters and climbed to altitude. As we climbed through the cloud cover, we emerged into a mass of twenty-eight bombers and sixty-four fighters. I wanted a fight, but these odds were ridiculous. I headed for the bombers, going through their formation, when a few Zeros bounced us from altitude out of the cloud bank above us. Then I sort of just grayed out. I was in a fog, but in my headset, I heard, "Pull out! Pull out!" The voice was my wingman, Greg Loesch. I opened my eyes and saw a large green mountain coming up at me, and I pulled back on the stick as hard as I could. I started climbing, and then realized that my oxygen mask had become unhooked. I was suffering from hypoxia and almost died as a result. I was lucky that my radio was working at that time, or I would not be here.

By the time the two of us got back to altitude, the fight was over. Everyone was going their separate ways, so we returned to the airfield. We landed and then got ready for another mission to escort some SBDs that were patched up and fueled. We could hear the ground battle; it sounded like it was next door. We took off and flew high cover over the bombers. We saw the five Jap transports and they were off-loading supplies. Farther away, Jap destroyers started firing up at us. While we had their attention the dive-bombers hit the transports and destroyed two of them.

Now, I have to tell this story. General Geiger's personal Catalina [PBY] was converted into a torpedo bomber. His aide Major [Jack] Cram told the mechanic to rig that thing to be able to drop two torpedoes suspended under the wings. Then they loaded the seaplane with extra fifty-caliber machine guns, making it a flying destroyer. And then he [Cram] took off without any fighter escort, just alone to attack Japanese ships. Well, we had just landed when we heard the engines, and I saw this PBY coming in with four Zeros on its ass. The Wildcats coming in to land diverted and engaged, shooting down three of them.

Then this story gets even crazier. That PBY still had one Zero on its tail coming into our airfield, blowing oily smoke from the port engine, when one of my pilots, Roger Haberman, was just about to touch down, gear extended. He saw this sideshow and pulled back on the stick as the PBY and Zero both passed by him. He just banked over and fired and the Zero exploded into a fireball. That was some exciting shit to watch, I can tell you, and that was his first kill.

You have to remember that most of the aerial fighting around Guadalcanal took place within twenty miles of Henderson Field. Between pilots in the air, naval vessels at sea, infantry on the ground, coast watchers, and the occasional gun camera film, confirming our kills was very easy to do. Very few claims were not confirmed. There were just too many eyeballs in the area. Haberman's kill right over the airfield was one of the easiest to confirm. When we looked at his Wildcat, it was full of holes and needed a paint job.

Major Cram was very thankful for Haberman's assistance, and then we were handed our new orders: unless we had enemies coming in at squadron strength, we were not to take off to engage, due to limited fuel. The ground gunners were to deal with them. Geiger wrote Cram up for a Navy Cross as a result of his unauthorized solo mission. The Japs lost two transports and four Zeros, and Geiger lost his personal aircraft that was too damaged to fly. I guess he thought that was a great trade-off. Not to be outdone, Geiger himself flew a dive-bomber to pay the Japs on the ground a visit. I guess to boost morale.

Then I became sick. I was shitting all the time and shaking with fever. I was not alone. I think every man there had dysentery and malaria. I laid down to take a nap one afternoon and woke up three days later in the makeshift hospital tent. That was when I was told that I had malaria. I looked around and saw a dozen guys on cots all around me, and the doc looked at me and waved his hand in a wide arc. "Relax, Foss. You are in very good company." I had to smile at that one. Then I threw up.

I was pleased that air transport felt secure enough in our abilities to send some supply flights in with much-needed fuel and ammunition. This was welcome since we had a ground attack mission to run, escorting the dive-bombers. We took off and hugged the ridgelines, skirting the hillsides, staying low to locate the Jap ground force. We found them and strafed the living hell out of them and then the dive-bombers packed a wallop. I believe the end result was that several hundred Jap soldiers were killed, and dozens of heavy artillery pieces were put out of action, for the loss of one dive-bomber and no fighters.

One thing the Japs would do sometimes is send a few fighters over to get us in the air. They had great range from their base in Rabaul, and they would try to lure us away from the airfield so their bombers could hit us unopposed. Being the operations officer, I always held a few fighters in reserve. I never wanted all the birds up at one time in case we got tangled up with those guys. At least we could radio back that we saw incoming bombers and those guys could take off and greet them on the way in. Bombers would usually be twenty minutes behind the Zekes, giving our guys plenty of time to get airborne. Often the Jap bombers would have their own fighter escorts to engage us and allow the bombers to hit Henderson Field.

My superiors found out about my hiding those extra Wildcats, and they were less than happy about it. The colonel called me in and gave me the rundown. We had to meet the general [Brigadier General Francis P. Mulcahy] and we did. The general poured some scotch, so I defended my position. He was in complete belief that the Japs had been reduced in number to the point that they were no longer an air threat. I countered, asking him what we would do if the reports were wrong. We would be caught unprepared at the most critical air base in the Solomon Islands.

I spent about three hours with my colonel, defending my position in holding those fighters in reserve, based upon what we saw in the air. I also explained that although we were seeing fewer fighters, we were seeing newer aircraft. You could tell—aircraft in combat get damaged, patched up, weathered, and just plain worn out. We were seeing freshly painted and pristine fighters. The general wanted all the planes on missions, believing G2 [intelligence] that the Japs were done in the air. But I was not buying it. I believed the Japs had not retreated, but were massing for a main thrust.

[Hideki] Tojo also knew how critical Guadalcanal was, as did General Vandegrift, [General] MacArthur, and Admiral Halsey. That was why they kept throwing landing craft and infantry on the beaches. They wanted Henderson Field back. We had to hold on to that rock at all costs. If the Japs knocked us off and took it back, they would dominate the South Pacific and we would have been royally screwed. Well, with that opinion, I was told that I was fired and to basically get the hell out of his office.

After that was said and done, I went back to the guys and told them what had happened. We would be going home more than likely, or at the very least reassigned to a noncombat role somewhere. Probably as flight instructors. The depression that set in was clear. The next morning, a somber gathering just hung around the fighters at the end of the strip, bullshitting basically. We had other fighter squadrons there and we alternated flying missions, a staggered schedule to keep a CAP [combat air patrol] over the field. There was a primitive radar set, and coast watchers were worthless in sighting the incoming enemy aircraft when your warning time was about five minutes on a good day.

I was smoking one of my trademark cigars, laughing at something, when the radar operator on a ship picked up some aircraft around Savo Island, not far away. The office of the watch and the NCO line chief both said no, we had no one in that area. I knew right then that the Japs were going to vindicate me, so we saddled up and took off into what I knew was going to be a fight. We took eight Wildcats and hit twelve thousand feet looking for the incoming bandits. Then we had a radio call that four more fighters were taking off to join in the hunt.

I called the Zeros out far below us—about a dozen if I recall—and they seemed to be doing crazy things, like an air show. I suspected they were the bait to get us to come down; then we would get bushwhacked. I radioed the guys to keep their eyes upward and gain altitude and keep looking around. This did not feel right. Jap pilots were not stupid creatures. They had a lot more combat experience than we did, and if you underestimated one, you did so with your head up your ass. We weaved back and forth to keep an eye on our tails as well.

We were below the clouds and in the middle of a very large number of Japanese aircraft. That turned out to be something like more than a hundred enemy planes—Bettys, over sixty Zeros, and eighteen to twenty Val dive-bombers. There was no doubt in my mind where they were headed. I then hit the radio and called it in the clear. That alerted the remaining ground fighters to get airborne and pick up the incoming stragglers after we hit them. I knew that if I had not kept fighters down, ready for a defensive takeoff, it would have been ugly.

We did a lot of strafing as well, hitting troops in the open, trucks, anything with a military signature and of value. I once blew up a gas truck, pretty spectacular. When we had coordinates from ground troops or an aerial observation, we would plot these attacks. The great thing about the Marine Corps is that we use aviation officers, pilots, working with the infantry and artillery units. They function as forward air controllers and observers. Their skill as pilots provides a unique perspective to bringing aerial ordnance down on bad guys on time and on target. We were guided in many times by these ground controllers and to great effect.

We had word that the USS *Hornet* task force was offshore, and that would mean greater support and supplies, as they had a force of fighters, dive-bombers, and torpedo bombers. That was both a blessing and a curse. We had a small supply ship in the mouth of the Lunga River with about forty thousand gallons of badly needed gas, oil, and ammunition. Well, a flight of Japanese Val bombers found it and attacked. They killed a few sailors, and we lost that precious cargo. The only good part of that was when VMF-212 showed up led by Lieutenant Colonel Joe [Harold William "Indian Joe"] Bauer. They caught up with the enemy formation and downed four of them.

The next morning was one for the diary. I woke up hearing gunfire and stepped outside of my tent. Looking up, I saw an air battle: a Zero spinning on fire, and Wildcats led by our CO,

Duke Davis, and his flight were dogfighting less than four hundred feet over my tent. I just watched the show. I saw them flame six bombers and four Zeros, easy kills to confirm, as I said before. There was nowhere on that green-ass rock where you could not see an air battle, unless you were deep in the jungle. Then we had our mission.

One of our problems was that we were getting bombed or shelled so often that not all of the holes could be patched up in time. This was to be one of those times. We were taking off when Andy Andrews, who had been with me on the big landing-craft-strafing mission, must have hit one of those shell holes, and lost control and crashed into another parked Wildcat. The explosion was brilliant. We lost Andy, one of the mechanics was badly hurt, and others had minor injuries, I believe. That was a very depressing way to start a mission, and our last two pilots had to wait to take off until the wreckage was cleared away. We circled, waiting for them to climb up to us after take-off. I banked and looked over and saw that those two guys were being chased by three Zeros, and it looked as if the Wildcat pilots were not aware of the danger.

I continued my roll and dove in with my flight. When I recovered, I was behind the Zeros. I picked the one on my far left and lit his ass up and he spun in. The tracers I fired that missed the Zero flashed by the Wildcats and alerted the two pilots who were now aware that they had an issue. Then I saw another Zero that had rolled over to dive away. I did not follow that, but I turned to see where he went, and when he leveled out, I went in. This guy was good. He managed to jink around and slip away even as I was closing on him. I then pulled lead and fired, and I saw smoke from his engine, but I did not get a confirmed kill. I was still moving my head around to make sure I was not jumped by another one of his teammates. There were Wildcats and Zeros swirling all around above me; it really was a brawl.

Then this other Zero came at me head-on, firing way out of range. He was jerking around, then trying to slip under me, so I held my fire. We came closer and passed each other. Then I looked over my left shoulder and saw him pull a hard right turn like he was headed home. I dropped the nose and went right rudder and closed the distance. We both banked and did it all over again and then I fired. He broke up and went into the ocean.

That was the thing about the Japs: they flew as independent units, not as a team or in anything resembling an attack formation. We flew in two four-ship formations, the "finger four" that we adopted from the British. They had stolen it from the Germans, who started using it in the Spanish Civil War. [*The "Finger Four" was developed by Luftwaffe ace Werner Mölders in 1937 and became flying-combat doctrine for the rest of the war. All the Allied nations copied the tactic.*]

That was when I saw another Zero chasing a Wildcat. I turned to get him, but he saw me, broke off the Wildcat he was chasing, and then turned in to me head-on. At the last second, the Jap pulled up and away. I had a great deflection shot, but then saw a Wildcat behind the Zero, so I did not fire. I was afraid of hitting one of my own men. I looked right and behind me and saw a formation of eight Bettys with their Zeros, so I banked high and right into a climb, reversing on a one-hundred-eighty-degree course, and lined up on the nearest bomber. I was diving on him when he exploded. I knew that someone else got him.

I had to avoid the debris from that bomber as I lined up another one, but I was too close to it for a long burst, so I fired a quick one and saw hits. I flew down past the formation, converting altitude into airspeed, and then pulled up to get altitude for another run on them. I was still climbing when I lined up the belly of a Betty. I was almost stalling in a vertical climb, leading the bomber when I fired. I was perhaps less than two hundred feet away from it when the gas tank flashed and the Betty became a torch.

I could feel the heat as I stalled and began to fall back to earth. The bomber fell away, shedding parts all over the place. It went right past me as I was falling, and I could watch the whole show. Then the wing exploded and separated. The bomber twirled into the ocean, and no one from the bomber's crew got out. I noticed that all the remaining bombers and Zeros were gone when my engine died. Now I had to return in a dead-stick landing without power. I had a little damage but nothing major. But when I landed, I knew that I was officially an ace. I was congratulated on the ground because all the kills we made had been confirmed from the ground.

I once had another emergency landing when I took off in a

dead-lined Wildcat. I asked the crew chief why it was down, and he said that the pilot claimed it had a bad magneto reading or something. Well, I decided to take it up and see for myself. I started it and it sputtered and coughed a bit, but I had power for takeoff. I got that sucker up, but I read the instruments and knew I would never clear the trees past the runway, so I banked it around below a hundred feet to return when the engine just died. I saw all that green below me and I just knew that this was not going to be good.

Well, the prop clipped a tree, and that spun me into another. I was thrust forward against the seat straps and banged the hell out of my head. One tree took the landing gear and shattered the canopy and another took the right wing, while the rest of the wreckage crumpled to the ground with me in it, which woke me up. I crawled out of that thing as fast as I could, being afraid of fire.

As if to add insult to injury, Jap bombers then showed up and began hitting us again. I saw a lot of blood from a head wound when I took my helmet off, and there was a hole in it from the shattered glass. The doc arrived with the ambulance. I was sitting nearby in a trench and waved that I was OK. Then I had my ass reamed by Joe Bauer for even taking that plane up due to the dead-line repair order.

Then we learned that Admiral "Bull" Halsey was taking over direct command of Guadalcanal and the Solomons campaign. More good news for us was the arrival of a fresh crop of new pilots, and with them all the wonderful contraband from the

States back home. We had coffee, chocolate, beer, a few bottles of scotch, canned meat, you name it. We felt like it was Christmas. Not long after that, I went to the front and took a lot of the food and stuff with me. Those guys had seen nothing and eaten even less for several weeks. I was surprised to learn that I was somewhat famous now.

I looked at those grunts, unshaven, with hollow eyes and gaunt faces. If God ever chose men to be his warriors, I was looking at them. I sat down with them, and we talked about what was happening, catching up on scuttlebutt, that kind of shit. Mail call was the highlight and I got letters from Mom and June, and they were welcomed. The chaplains would make the rounds, even going into a hot zone to hold services. I always thought that was pretty damned brave, because you would see a Catholic priest dressed in white giving communion in a jungle where everything was green. He stood out like a pink elephant, a great target for Jap snipers. But they went in and did their jobs, giving comfort to those men, many of them teenagers in their first time away from home and seeing death every day. I will never forget their faces, and how happy they were that a now "famous" ace thought enough of them to bring them gifts. That memory will always stay with me. God bless those grunts. They had been through hell and saved our asses.

I also wondered if I bailed out if I would get strafed in my parachute. We had heard about it, and I only knew of one of our pilots who did that to a Jap, and he received a very severe reprimand, as it violated the Geneva Convention, to which we were a signatory nation. That guy did it again but was killed himself. That was not the way we conducted war. Besides, the G2 types wanted a live pilot for interrogation as opposed to a corpse. There had been a few—I mean, very few—Jap prisoners taken on Guadalcanal, but whatever value they had for us was unknown to me.

I mentioned Joe Conger, a great guy and childhood friend. He was a very aggressive pilot, and a good one, and a great story involves October 25, 1942, when eight Zekes hit Henderson Field, and Joe was one of the four Wildcats in the air engaging them. He was involved with some shit-hot pilots, and that fight lasted at least five minutes. That is an eternity in fighter combat. I was with the others watching from the ground when he pulled up into a Zero and used his propeller to cut through the fuselage right behind the cockpit, destroying both fighters. Both pilots bailed out at around fifteen hundred feet. They had good parachutes and both landed in the water offshore.

The sailors took a boat to go get the Jap pilot, but he pointed to Joe about fifty yards away, so they went to get Conger first. They reeled him in and then went for the Jap. They pulled him in, but then he pulled his pistol, aimed it at Joe, and pulled the trigger. It misfired. Then he cleared it and tried to shoot himself in the head and again—*click*, a misfire. Joe had had enough of that shit and he clocked the Jap with a gas can, knocking him out. That was our first enemy prisoner.

The best part of this story was that the Jap pilot, Shiro Ishikawa, later met Conger at a reunion back in 1990. They actually became friends. I know people wonder how that can happen, but it does. We all know Saburō Sakai. He was the top-scoring Japanese ace to survive the war, and we all love that guy. He always believed in fighting honorably, and he really got into some trouble back home by demanding that the Japanese government start acknowledging the war crimes they had never admitted to. Hell, they even claimed that no crimes were ever committed.

Sakai openly challenged that position, demanding that Japan follow Germany's example of admitting that crimes against humanity occurred, and we all admired him for it. Ironically, Sakai says I am the best friend he has in the United States, and I take that as a very high honor. He is a very good man. It was a tragedy that our nations had to fight each other, and he agrees with me.

One memorable day was November 7, when we crept up on a flight of Zeros, including some pontoon versions for water operations. They were chasing another flight, and we were behind the Japs at a higher altitude. I got behind one and fired, and his fighter just disintegrated in the explosion. My wingman [Boot Furlow] hit another and knocked it down. The most disturbing part of this engagement was that we lost a great Irishman, Danny Doyle.

He had just lost his best friend, [Carey] Brandon. They were both from Minnesota, and Brandon's death hit him hard, so I grounded him for a while. I wanted his head clear. Well, this was his first sortie since then, and I should have known better. I saw Doyle head straight into a Zero. The collision blew both aircraft apart, killing both men. I felt guilty that I had let him fly so soon. I second-guessed myself as to whether or not I did the right thing. If he was going to commit suicide to kill a Jap, I told myself, then it could have happened at any time. But still, it was hard. I dealt with it. There would be a lot more death before the war was over, and some were good friends.

But that happened while in combat, so I had to set it aside and focus on the task at hand. This was a real rodeo, I will tell you. I rolled over to get back into the fight, but it was already over. All the Japs were destroyed. What was crazy was that there were five empty parachute harnesses, and I saw the sixth one with the pilot still in it. He then released the harness and fell to his death, passing right by me. I found this extraordinary. I began to learn more about the Bushido code. I admired their dedication, but I questioned their application of it.

This same mission saw us hit some Jap ships trying to run the slot. I saw one of the floatplanes out of the corner of my eye, so I decided to take him out to cover the rest of the group. I climbed into the clouds to get above him and then looked down, and there he was. What I thought was a single-seat float-plane was in fact a two-seater and a slow-moving target. When I dove in, I had to pull away to avoid a collision. The pilot was well aware of me, and he also banked, and his rear gunner put rounds through my canopy in front of my face and into the left-engine cowling.

I told the rest to continue their attack against the ships. Then I caught the Jap with a shot in his right wing that caught fire and he burned into the ocean. I saw his wingman up ahead and he seemed not even to know that he was all alone. I just closed the distance, pulled slightly up, and fired into his belly, and he headed down to the ocean. I saw the rest of the Wildcats were heading toward the ships, and I tried to radio my condition, but had no response. I assumed that my radio had died, which seemed to be a regular problem for me. However, in case I could be heard, I still transmitted. Perhaps the receiver was damaged, but the transmitter was working.

Then my worst nightmare happened. Once again, I had an engine sputter out and almost die. My entire flight had done their job and were headed back. I had no way to communicate, no engine power—I was all alone in a bad piece of airspace. I started to sweat. The only noise I heard was the wind rushing into my shattered canopy, nothing else, not even radio static. That was a strange feeling. Then the engine restarted from the sputter, and I saw another Wildcat. He was flying even slower than I was, so I caught up to him.

I ran into a rain squall and lost sight of the other Wildcat, which I had recognized as Jake Stub. But when I came through the clouds, I could not see him. My engine sputtered again as I was flying into another wall of rain, and then it just up and died for good. I looked ahead at a couple of islands and checked my compass, and realized I was off course to return home. I was losing altitude, looking at the vast ocean and remembering that I never learned to swim. [*Stub was shot down by a flight of Zeros who were chasing Foss, but they lost him in the clouds. Foss never even knew they were there. Stub bailed out and returned to Henderson Field five days later.*]

I had thirteen thousand feet of altitude, and I locked onto an island that was just east of me. We had inflatable Mae West life jackets, but I knew that any air rescue would be impossible, even if they could fly. Besides, the sharks would probably get me sooner than later. Well, I spotted some beach that I thought might be a good place to slide into and started to circle around. But I screwed up and was losing altitude faster than anticipated. I was going into the drink about five miles from shore. Add to that, the storm that was building. I was not very reassured about my chances.

I slid the canopy back and prepared to climb out quickly before the plane sank. But once again, instead of sliding onto the surface and riding it out, the tail struck and then bounced up, forcing the nose into the water at high velocity. The force of the impact slammed the canopy forward and closed it on me. Water gushed into the cockpit from the broken glass, and the plane sank like a rock. Then I remembered that I had violated two cardinal rules of a water landing: I failed to jettison the canopy and release the parachute harness so I could get out safely.

I was in complete darkness, having become a submarine, and I managed to hit the canopy release. I was swallowing water as I was struggling, and then managed to release the parachute straps. I hit the air cylinders to inflate the Mae West and was pulled upward out of the cockpit. The parachute assisted taking me to the surface, but ass up and head down, so breathing was still not an option. Then I suddenly stopped moving upward, and felt my left foot get stuck under the seat. I had to reach down and free it manually, starved for air, but when I did, I flew to the surface ass first with my head still underwater.

I managed to release one of the parachute harness straps, then struggled to get the other one to use as additional flotation, but I had to tighten the Mae West straps because they had come loose, and the Mae West was going over my head. I do not know how deep I had gone down with the plane, but it must have been a good depth. If I had to guess, I would say my ascent took at least a minute. As I broke surface and could breathe, I thought I had probably set a world record for a human being holding his breath. I had swallowed a good bit of seawater but being able to breathe was the most precious thing of all.

I also knew that I had to swim, or I would die out there, and to do that, I needed to get rid of excess weight. I dumped my boots to lighten my load, but then immediately realized that I had been an idiot. The small coral reef atoll around the beaches would cut my feet up badly. Then I thought about two positives: I was not dead, and I was not wounded and bleeding, which would have been bad for a variety of reasons. With the darkness closing in and the current seeming to be carrying me out to sea, I was not feeling any better. Then, in the dimming daylight, I saw the shark fin. I guess you could say that depression set in.

We had these chlorine vials that we were to break as shark repellent. I found out years later that those damned things did not work. I started praying and thought about Dad, friends, everything. But then I heard voices and got really scared. If they were Japs, I was done for. I saw a light coming closer, and the people turned out to be natives in a dugout canoe with a Catholic priest, Father Dan Stuyvenberg, and another white man named Tommy Robertson coming to pull me out. I really owed those guys. They saw me go in and came out to see if I survived. I thought that was very polite of them.

When we reached the beach, there was a large fire and a large group of people there, clergy from all over the world. Bishops, priests, nuns, all of them had escaped other islands when the Japs invaded and managed to reach this one, Malaita, much to my good fortune. As we spoke, I heard about the atrocities the Japs had committed against these priests, nuns, and civilians, including murder and rape. To me it was unbelievable how terrible people could be to each other.

By the way, I spoke about this event and others with Saburō and he said he was very disappointed in the conduct of his country's soldiers. That meant a lot to the Americans, and even Australians who got together [at reunions]. He was a stand-up guy.

They were all interested in learning what was going on. Due to their isolation, the only source of information they had was from Robertson's small radio. One of the older sisters had been on her island for something like forty years. They saw the air battles and airplanes but were clueless as to the extent of the greater war raging around them. I told them all I could. I was also in heaven because they fed me steaks, eggs, milk, bread, fish, and fruits. They even gave me dry clothes to wear so I could get out of my soaked flight gear. By the way, this was the best meal that I had enjoyed in several months, despite still being sick from the seawater I had ingested. When I laid down to sleep, I think I went into a coma, I was so exhausted.

When I woke up, I heard singing. My head was pounding, probably from the seawater. They had built a church—well, a hut really, rigged with religious relics and such. There were a bunch of native islanders. There were some real characters, like something out of a Tarzan movie with necklaces, loincloths, you name it. One of the priests said they had been headhunters and fierce warriors but they were now Christians and adopted into the Catholic Church. I found that fascinating. He also said they hated the Japs. That made me feel better also.

Father Dan took care of me, and I really appreciated that. Then we heard an airplane overhead, so I ran into a clearing. It was a Wildcat. The pilot banked, and we saw each other. He was low and I clearly identified him as one of our pilots, Dutch Bruggeman. He waved and waggled his wings, so I knew I would get picked up. A few hours later, a Catalina landed at sea and started cruising in near the shore. I said goodbye to those fine people and promised that I would inform military authorities as to their location and situation. Then two natives paddled me out to the PBY. It looked familiar. When I boarded, I discovered that the pilots were Jack Cram and Charles Parker, flying General Geiger's repaired PBY. I told them of the event during the flight back to Guadalcanal.

When I arrived, I was treated like a celebrity. They had all thought I was dead for certain. They updated me on what had happened, the men we lost, and I told them about the island and the people there. I remember writing all that down in my diary before I went to sleep. I was glad to be back with the guys but sad at the losses.

The next morning, I got up and joined Bill Freeman and Wally [Wallace] Wethe for an awards ceremony. Admiral Halsey read our citations and awarded us each the Distinguished Flying Cross. Then he gathered all the pilots together. I guess to smooth any hard feelings we may have had with the Navy for not stopping the Japs from shelling us from the sea. Admiral Nimitz needed aggressive leaders in the fleet, and he had appointed Halsey. Now that he was in charge, he promised things would be different. After a mission the next day, I flew over Malaita, where I had been rescued. I had packed a duffel bag with all kinds of food and rigged it to the plane. As I flew over, I released the rope and dropped that stuff to my friends.

[On November 11, 1942,] Boot Furlow and I took off on a two-ship sweep, looking for a Jap flying boat. We did not see it, but after we got back, the entire unit was scrambled to intercept about fifty Japs flying toward Halsey's fleet. There was not enough gas to get us in the air, so he and I took a truck and drove around, looking for gas. We struck gold and found a gas truck, and took it back to fill up, but we had lost a lot of time. The rest of the group were long gone. When we lifted off, I was glad to see that my radio was working, as I could hear the voices during the action. They had slammed right into a serious fight, and it sounded critical. I could hear what was happening and there was nothing we could do to help. They shot down eleven Japs but lost seven planes and five pilots in the process. My heart sank at that news, I can tell you.

The surviving casualties included our CO, Duke, with shrapnel wounds in his right torso and face, and Roger Haberman, who had a Jap shell that entered under his fuselage also enter his thigh and continue all the way until it lodged near his scrotum. They saved his life despite the massive amount of blood he lost and patched him up enough to get him to the main hospital at Espiritu Santo. We all thought he was going home, a million-dollar wound and retirement. Well, you will not believe this, but a few days later, he showed up, limping badly, back at Henderson Field. He was dressed in his flight suit and said he was ready to go. I knew that was bullshit, but I humored him. I was just surprised that the hospital released him. Well, there's more on that story.

The next day [November 12, 1942], we took off after a coast watcher reported a flight of Betty bombers inbound. We perched at twenty-nine thousand feet to have great visibility and a quick bounce on the formation, classic tactics. We had ships out there, a couple of transports and a few destroyers, so that was probably their target. We saw them coming in far below, just five hundred feet off the ocean. From nearly six miles up, you can see a lot when the sky is clear.

We peeled over and screamed in at full throttle. My airspeed indicator read six hundred knots—twice what Grumman suggested in their operations manual. The inside of the cockpit frosted over, and I heard it crack from the pressure. Our unit as well as other Wildcats were joined by P-39 Airacobras from the Army [67th Fighter Squadron] as we all flew through the thick flak thrown up by all of our ships. My group ended up right behind the bombers and began hitting them long before they could reach the ships. My first kill was about a hundred yards ahead of me. I was closing fast when I fired, and the right engine caught fire and went into the sea. I was lining up on another one when a Zero jumped me from above, but he overshot, so I pulled up and nailed him, and he was gone. He hit the water and broke apart and scattered all over the surface.

Then I turned my attention back to the first bomber I was trying to nail, and managed to hit him in the wing root. The fire and flash told me those were good hits, so he was done. After landing we received the report that it was a clean sweep and the ships had not been touched. Starting the next day, and over the next few days, we got a lot of aircraft joining us at Henderson Field. The Cactus Air Force grew. We were getting Army P-38 and P-39 units, an Army B-25 unit, more Wildcats, more SBDs [Dauntless dive-bombers], TBF Avengers [torpedo bombers].

We received deliveries of bombs, torpedoes, and more ammunition for the fighters than I had ever seen. We also had a large influx of additional maintenance personnel and gasoline supplies. I knew that something big was coming, and not long after midnight on November 13, every siren on the island went off. We knew what to expect. I looked for the closest foxhole, but the bombers never came. But I could hear naval guns in the distance, and the skyline was lit up as bright as day. That meant the Japs were engaging our fleet, and an invasion to retake the island was underway. They had to neutralize our airpower to support their amphibious landings.

[*The Japanese Imperial Navy sent the battleships* Hiei *and* Kirishima *with eleven destroyer escorts and a light cruiser to bombard the island, and in particular Henderson Field. They were engaged by eight American destroyers and five cruisers in what would become known as the Naval Battle of Guadalcanal, one of six naval battles fought for that island.*]

I took off at first light to get a view of what was going on. I saw something I will never forget off Lunga Point. Ships were burning, ours and theirs. I spotted what turned out to be the Jap battleship *Hiei* with three destroyers. It was badly damaged, and I knew that our bombers could finish it off. I radioed back what I saw, and as soon as I landed, I was refueled, and all the other aircraft were ready to go. The plan was for the fighters to dive in and blaze away to get their attention. Then the torpedo bombers would come around Savo Island and strike them. Then we would again strafe and divert their attention as the dive-bombers came in to finish the job. That battleship was the primary target.

I led my group and rolled over into about a seventy-degree dive, firing as I went. I closed fast and had to raise my left wing as I pulled out to avoid hitting the ship, followed by my men. I knew that we would do little damage, but that was not the objective. Their attention was on us, and the amount of fire that came up was incredible, but I was not hit. Then we headed back to base and General Geiger was there waiting for us. The initial reports were promising, so he wanted us to go back for another round. We did, repeated the same mission, and when it was over, newspapers were reporting that the first Jap battleship sunk was done with the support of Marine and Navy aircraft. We all felt proud, but we also had to take in the losses suffered by the Navy.

That was humbling, and after I saw what they went through, I felt guilty for bad-mouthing the Navy when they failed to secure our supply lines and provide us with what we needed. Over a thousand sailors gave their lives. One of our mechanics lost his brother on the USS *Portland*, if memory serves. As he was the sole surviving son, I saw to it that the paperwork was done to get him home to his widowed mother. That woman had lost enough in this life, in my opinion. General Geiger readily approved the paperwork. That was the least we could do. I was really starting to hate that damned war.

But the Japs were not done. That very night our old friend flew overhead and dropped a few small bombs, but then we got pounded by more Jap naval gunfire, and we lost two Wildcats. At sunrise we were up and pretty pissed off. We were determined to hurt them badly. We fighters flew cover for the bombers, and [Lieutenant] Colonel Joe Bauer wanted to go. His duties kept him on the ground, but he was determined to get involved. He was a real Marine. We were ready to get going, but Bauer's fighter would not kick over, so I told Loesch to take the flight and [Boot] Furlow and I would join up once the colonel was good to go.

Well, by the time the three of us were on our way, we encountered our squadron returning from their strike, and we could see five of the eight Jap transport ships burning. Bauer decided we would go in and do some damage as well, rather than head back with the group. We roared in in a wave formation just six feet above the water, hoping to keep below their deck-gun depression while pumping thousands of rounds into the ships. Then came the Zeros. Bauer scored one in a turn as he flashed past him while I chased another one, weaving through the smoking transports. I can only imagine what the Jap sailors were thinking as they watched the show.

I was on the tail of one Zero, but had to break contact and pull up to avoid colliding into a transport, so he got away. But then another Zero arrived and it was an easy shoot down. When I fired, I looked over and saw Furlow get a kill. My radio had gone out again and I formed up with Boot and gave him the hand signal for "no communication." He nodded his head—he was used to it. We looked around for Bauer and saw a large oil slick in the water. We flew low and he waved us off, so we flew back. Boot radioed the situation, so when we arrived the Duck [single-engine amphibious rescue aircraft] was ready to go. I climbed in the bottom as Colonel [Joe] Renner started to taxi. We were getting up some speed when a B-25 rolled right in our path, which I could not see. Renner barely managed to clear the bomber. Then the Duck dipped and pulled up, and he just managed to clear a tree. I had no idea what was going on. I was just being bounced around below in the hold. After we were safely airborne, I climbed up in the cockpit. He just looked at me and shook his head. I guided him to where we last saw Bauer swimming.

We were scanning the water as the sun went down, but it got dark fast, and we could not see anything except the glow of burning ships. We were just off the ocean surface, the water illuminated by the fires in the distance and searchlights from the Japs as they apparently looked for their own men in the water. We almost collided with a blacked-out Jap destroyer. I suggested we go back and try again at first light, since we couldn't see anything. My fears were that Bauer had either drowned or been killed by a shark, or the Japs had got him. I know Renner was thinking the same thing, but we did not discuss it.

The next morning, I skipped breakfast and got men in the air to fly back ahead of the rescue Duck. We saw that the ships had sunk and there was shit all over the water. Floating bodies, garbage, everything you could imagine that would not sink was bobbing up and down. Then we were jumped by six Zeros. In a matter of three minutes or so, they were all shot down. We continued our search, ready to radio for the rescue Duck, but had to return to base empty-handed. Joe Bauer was listed as MIA and he was never seen again. That was a hard blow to us because he was one of the most respected men on that island. No one said much after we returned. We all missed him. He left a wife and young son behind also.

[*Lieutenant Colonel Harold William Bauer (November 20, 1908–November 14, 1942) was finally listed as killed in action on January 8, 1946, and credited with eleven victories, of which ten could be confirmed from after-action reports. Foss witnessed Bauer shooting at two. He did not see them crash, but saw they were definitely damaged. Due to his record and the fact he had volunteered for that last mission, Bauer's nomination for the Navy Cross was upgraded at the request of General Roy Geiger, and he was posthumously awarded the Medal of Honor and Purple Heart.*]

Then we got a message from the military police that Haberman was charged with going AWOL [absent without leave]. I asked him about that, and he openly admitted that he just limped out of the hospital and managed to bullshit his way onto one of the transports coming back. I laughed at the audacity of it, but we had to smooth it over. We got it worked out so he would not go to the brig. Personally, the malaria and dysentery along with the medication turned me yellow, but I was not alone. Many of us suffered with chills and fevers. Finally, they rotated us out to New Caledonia for some much-needed R and R [rest and recuperation]. We were exhausted after three solid months of operations. It felt good to get a solid night's sleep without worrying about Maytag Charlie, air raids, or getting shelled from the sea. The food was also a lot better.

Then another situation arose when the military police contacted me to say that they had arrested seven of my guys for being out of uniform. I needed a favor, so I went to Admiral Halsey's office. He had said if I ever needed anything to ask—well, there I was. What had happened was, the guys were having their uniforms cleaned and decided to wear some Aussie shorts and shirts, but with their [U.S.] rank and wings. Halsey called the officer in charge of the military police and had the men brought to his office. When he saw them, he just laughed. Halsey was to the Navy what Omar Bradley was to the Army. He was a real leader, able to sit down and eat chow with an enlisted man as if it was a natural thing, no bluster, and we had many get-togethers over the years until he died. I really admired him.

I went to Sydney, Australia, for a couple of weeks and that was a great time. I went with old Finney, and I was able to hear more exciting and amazing stories about his life and the people he knew. I was amazed at how many dignitaries and Aussie celebrities knew him and came to see him. He was the real deal. The meals were also incredible: steaks all the time, fresh eggs, real milk, good beer, even single-malt scotch. Finney and I were treated like royalty. I remember telling him that I needed to hang out with him more often. He told me that I could be a movie star after the war, but I did not think that was something I could comfortably do. Years later I thought, "What the hell? Audie Murphy did it." I knew Audie, and he was a hard drinker like Boyington, but unlike Greg, he was a very nice and humble fellow.

Not long afterward, I learned that I was also famous there. I had been in the newspapers in Australia, along with other prominent Americans, for some time. There was a story attributed to me that was not true. As it went, the story was that I landed a Wildcat without wings. It started as a joke by another pilot and the press ran with it. So much for journalism.

I also want to tell you about when I met some Australian pilots who had fought in North Africa. I was trying like hell to get a chance to fly a Spitfire, as they had been famous fighters since 1940. I met Clive Caldwell, who they called "Killer Caldwell." The Australians had been sent back [to Australia] to fight the Japs now, and these guys wanted our information and experience on how to fight them. Likewise, I wanted to know about their experiences against the Germans. But these clowns seemed uninterested in learning our tactics in combat. They were more interested in the individual fighting abilities of the aircraft.

They asked me tactical questions, and I explained the methods we used again and again, and they still seemed disinterested. They were of the opinion that they would all be heroes since they were flying a fighter that was only two-thirds of the weight, faster, and more maneuverable than a Wildcat. I tried to tell them that the Thach Weave worked because it kept every gun covering every position in a dogfight protecting the formation while allowing us to engage any enemies coming in. Still, they yawned. Screw them, I said to myself. Learn the hard way. Well, they did. These guys went up and they had their collective asses handed to them in just a few missions because they tried the same shit that got them waxed in North Africa.

One thing I will say is that Caldwell was the one Aussie who listened intently to what I had to say while others just yawned and stared off into space. He later came to me to inquire privately. This guy was no damned joke—he was a true fighter pilot. He understood that there might be great differences in fighting styles in the Pacific and North Africa. He was definitely arrogant and confident, but he was no fool, and he wanted all the intel I had on Zeros—aerodynamics, armament, durability, pilot quality, that kind of stuff. Hell, he pulled out a pen and writing pad and took notes.

He wanted to know if Zeros were "dodgy" [of inferior quality]. He also spoke about flying with the "pommy bastards" [Englishmen] fighting the Germans in the war in North Africa.

He even mentioned that he knew the names of some of the Germans he had fought against. The name Marseille was mentioned a few times [Hans-Joachim Marseille]. After we were done, he called me a "bonzer bloke" [good guy] and said that a lot of his fellow pilots were "bludgers" [lazy and unmotivated] and "no hopers" [failures at life]. He thanked his American "cobbers" [friends] for helping keep Australia out of Jap hands. He then wanted to know if I would like a "butcher" [glass of beer] because he did not like to "drink with the flies" [drink alone] and that he was "gobsmacked" [surprised] at the news coming out about what happened at Guadalcanal. Now it was my turn to take notes.

He also said that many Australian soldiers and pilots considered us Americans "hoons" [hoodlums], "yobbos" [uncouth people], and "drongos" [idiots], but that we should just ignore the "knockers" [critics], because he knew all of that was "porky" [untrue]. Then he asked if we had "cracked onto" [romantically hit on] any of the better "moles" in town, meaning "hookers." I said no, of course not. I was married. Then Caldwell said, "Well, if you do crack onto one just use a condom on the 'old fella' [self-explanatory] because of the high rate of diseases."

I felt as if I was on another damned planet. I know we have some strange slang terms back in the States, regional vernacular and the like, but this shit was killing me, and I had to ask what the hell all of that meant. Caldwell, who did not seem to be a man with a very deep sense of humor, laughed his ass off when he saw the look on my face. I felt like I had just completed graduate school or been verbally mugged—I was not quite sure which. I looked at him [Finney] and said, "What the hell are you laughing at? You are just as confused as I am!" Finney replied, "Not exactly, I know all about covering the 'old fella'!"

He [Caldwell] admitted that he was not exactly a "wowser" [straitlaced puritan] himself. Then he produced a flask, unscrewed the top, and offered me a drink. I did not want to be rude, so I took a sip. It was the worst-tasting shit I ever swallowed. I would almost prefer seawater. I asked him what it was and he said, "Outback bourbon." For that one I did not need a translation, given my father's friendships with bootleggers. Later I heard Caldwell got into trouble smuggling illegal liquor, sort of like Al Capone, Lucky Luciano, and Joseph Kennedy back in the day, during Prohibition.

[*Caldwell was credited with 28.5 victories during the war, with 6.5 being Japanese victories, and he was the top Allied ace of the North African and Mediterranean Theaters. He was also the top scorer in the Curtiss P-40. Caldwell was court-martialed for smuggling alcohol from the Philippines into Morotai and running a black-market liquor business. He was reduced in rank from group captain (colonel) to flight lieutenant. After the war he became a successful businessman.*]

Later, after another long series of lectures where my advice fell on deaf ears, I was finally able to fly a Spitfire Mark IX. It was a marvelous aircraft to fly. The roll rate was better and the turning radius was also a little better [than the Wildcat]. Climbing was a dream, and the Rolls Merlin engine had a nice throaty roar but was much quieter than a Pratt and Whitney. On the downside, I could see right away that it was not as durable or well protected with armor plating as the Wildcat. It also had an inline engine as opposed to our radial, and it was a very smooth ride. I think I impressed them with my perfect three-point landing.

After that sojourn was over, I was cooling my heels on New Caledonia when I had the chance to speak with a captured Japanese fighter pilot and learn a few things. I also spent time reading through intelligence reports, catching up on what was going on. And, more important, trying to learn what might be coming. I got back to Henderson Field on New Year's Day, collected my mail, and talked with the guys. VMF-121 had almost ceased to exist as pilots were sent elsewhere to be the core of new units being built up. The old guys from my original flight were still there, and I met the new group commander, Lieutenant Colonel Sam Jack. He made me the squadron commander, so I had my old crew and a few new guys.

We had some new faces, replacement pilots, including a few Navy pilots who were homeless after their carrier sank and they landed on Henderson. I was happy to see that our fighter strip now had Marston Matting like the bombers had, which relieved us of having to repair the ground after the heavy rains. There had been no bombings for a couple of weeks, and they even had a big tent that showed all the Hollywood films. I got back into the routine and managed to sink a Jap boat, a wooden-hull spy ship that was transmitting, hidden under camo netting on the other side of the island. I stitched it up pretty good. The next day, only the mast was above the water, so I never knew if the crew was killed or jumped ship. If they jumped, they were probably in the hills with other Japs trapped on the island. I landed exhausted. I was still having the chills and joint ache from the malaria. It did not go away, but if I had complained, they would have taken me out of the action.

Well, the war got busy again. I clearly remember January 15, because we had a report that a PBY had spotted Jap ships, about five destroyers near the Russell Islands, and it had hit one on a bomb run. We scrambled and caught them with our dive-bombers with fighter escorts. The dive-bombers did good work and hit some; then the Zeros came in. The fight that followed cost us four Wildcats, but it cost the Japs eleven Zeros. Later that afternoon we took off with the dive-bombers again along with some Army P-39s. Two Jap ships had been spotted north of us, and we were going to pay them a visit. As soon as we saw them, we were engaged by Zeros.

I had not seen this type before. They had square wings, like the Wildcat. I knew that meant a better roll rate, and we had heard they could climb faster than the older model. Three of my men engaged them while the rest of us covered the dive-bombers. There was a second group of Zeros not that far away, just flying around, and that made me curious. I heard the victory calls over my working radio, and saw a few Zekes and a Wildcat minus a wing plunging down. I lined one up, but he maneuvered away from my shots, and then I had a Wildcat coming at me chased by bandits. I banked to get on their tails after the Wildcat passed by, but another Wildcat blew right down in front of me followed by a Zero, so I flamed him. He was only about fifty feet in front of me, an easy kill. I guessed that these new Zeros were just as flammable as the old ones.

Then I saw a Zero on the tail of the first Wildcat, which I learned was Oscar Bate, so I slipped to get a shot. But that Zero turned in to me head-on. We both started firing into each other. Neither one of us had good hits and we passed each other on our respective left sides, each banking to avoid the collision. The Zero made a turning climb and I climbed to meet him. Once again, we came at each other firing, and this time he broke high and right, giving me a split-second trigger squeeze. My rounds ripped into the unprotected cockpit area. I thought he was a goner. But hell no. This fool dove and then curved up in a fast climb to come back at me again.

He started smoking, but then his friends took an interest in me, so I decided that getting the hell out of there was better than trying to confirm a kill. As I banked away, I saw the Zero I had hit catch fire and then head into the ocean. I avoided the other Zeros and felt lucky until I was coming in to land and saw the airfield was under a bombing attack. "Great!" I thought. I was going to survive that crazy fight just to die landing on my own runway. I was low on fuel, empty really, but managed to set down. The Jap bombers left almost right away, and when I dismounted, I learned that the Wildcat I saw going in was my friend Bill Marontate.

Bill had shot down one Zero, then went head-to-head with another and their wings connected, which explained the spiraling F4F I saw. The Jap also went into the water. One of the tail gunners saw him [Bill] bail out. The after-action reports stated that there were six American parachutes. We hoped that he and the others could be rescued, but the Japs were a lot closer, and that depressed us. We flew a few missions to look for him and the others, but no luck. Bill was finally listed as missing in action along with the others. He was never heard from again, nor were the other men as far as I know. [*William Pratt Marontate was promoted to captain, posthumously awarded the Navy Cross and Purple Heart, and officially declared dead on February 15, 1945. He scored thirteen victories.*]

The only bright spot was when I was informed that I now had twenty-six victories, equaling Eddie Rickenbacker's World War I score. That was a benchmark every fighter pilot wanted. Oh, and our gunners finally got our friend from Maytag. He was shot down during one of his little nocturnal rendezvous. That lifted morale. I ended up spending more time in the operations side of the house, reading intel reports. I learned that our code breakers had once again performed their voodoo and our intel could now intercept the Japs at sea. That meant that they would not be able to reinforce their few remaining troops on the north end of Guadalcanal, basically dying on the vine. Good riddance, I thought, if true, but I had my doubts. I just could not believe that [Isoroku] Yamamoto was going to give up on our piece of paradise so easily. Everything I had learned about the man did not mesh with this new assessment.

Major General Francis P. Mulcahy was now in charge. I disagreed with his methods of running air operations, but I kept that to myself. I was thinking tactically. I knew that there were still Japs in the mountains, probably watching everything on the airfields, and more than likely, they had radios. I had little doubt that the Japs knew exactly what our status was. Mulcahy had a tendency to send our fighters on long flights that had stressed our range for little return, but that left us vulnerable to attack. We had new fighters and supplies, and they were not camouflaged. Planes sat on the apron in neat rows, a juicy target for any Jap to just shoot up. That was what I would do, so once again I hid eight Wildcats on the edge of the jungle and concealed from all eyes as a rapid response, should we have any unwanted visitors.

I spoke to Lieutenant Colonel Jack about my suspicions, and he agreed, but said he was going to play ignorant. It was on me; it was my squadron. I agreed. Well, the general found out and wanted me charged with failure to follow orders and misappropriation of military assets. He could not court-martial me due to my status with Admiral Halsey, General Geiger, and the American public, but he entered some remarks in my record that would basically kill any future promotions. I was basically in terminal pay grade after that, and he was shipping me out. Well, almost.

The next day my premonitions proved correct and Mulcahy looked like a fool. It was January 25 and I was getting ready for one of the ridiculous flights Mulcahy wanted, wasting fuel and time in case we were attacked. There had not been any reports of ships at all. Then a Navy pilot came up and asked me if any of our guys were flying around Savo Island. I knew what that meant. I told him no, ordered my guys up immediately, and took off. At eighteen thousand feet, we hit pay dirt.

We saw twelve Zeros down below. I ordered the flight to keep climbing, then radioed back for the second flight to take off and updated them. We were joined by four P-38 Lightnings who heard the chatter over their radios. We climbed up into the layered cloud banks, and I saw them—about sixty Zeros and over twenty Bettys. I radioed that back to the second flight also. The first dozen Zeros were the advance party, coming in to either hit the airfield and destroy the fighters, or lure them away from covering the base. That would have eliminated any aerial interdiction on our part. Then I radioed for the airfield to scramble everything to get them off the ground. I used a little profanity, which brought back a smart-ass remark from the radio operator.

I resisted the temptation to jump right in. I headed down onto a Zero, but thought better about it and pulled back up. I had to control myself. I needed to keep the Japs interested in us until the rest of the air element was in position. The Lightnings were the first to draw blood, taking out two Zekes that climbed up. The remaining Zeros from the advance party wanting to pick a fight turned back and headed home, probably low on fuel. The Bettys and remaining Zeros saw our aircraft, but they had no idea if our numbers were even greater due to the heavy cloud cover. They also aborted the mission and headed back. A P-38 pilot confirmed that they were retreating, which was highly unusual.

We landed back at the base, and I learned that General Mulcahy had heard everything. He knew I was right, and General Geiger showed up soon after that and congratulated me on such a great defensive preparation. Mulcahy could do nothing to me after that. Geiger was the senior officer in that area of operations. Then we started getting a massively heavy rainstorm that killed visibility on the ground to about two hundred feet. No Japs would be coming back through that.

To his credit, Colonel Jack did not try to take credit for disobeying the order that I had disobeyed; he just gently reminded Mulcahy that I saved the base. Then it was decided that my flight and Major John Smith's would be rotated out. Smith had applied to extend his tour, but he was denied. I knew better than to even ask, since Mulcahy, despite writing a glowing report of the action and my actions under his command, still wanted me gone. I knew when to not push a bad position. My days on Guadalcanal were over.

What I did not know was that Geiger had written me up for

the Medal of Honor, but had not sent the request through all the proper channels. Generally speaking, that recommendation normally goes up the chain of command far below the rank of general, but somewhere along the way, Mulcahy was kept out of the communications loop. Before I left, Geiger gave me some wisdom, and he asked me if I needed anything. I asked if I could get a regular commission, as I was just a reservist. He said no problem; he could take care of it. Then he told me that I would be put on national display as a war hero. So just get used to it, play it right, mingle at the cocktail parties, and hob-nob with the right people who wanted photographs taken with me. He said for me to expect to be placed on a war bonds drive with celebrities. It was all part of the program.

I boarded the transport plane and flew off, realizing I would soon be home. I had to wait on Espiritu Santo for a ship, but I spent time with Commander James Flatley, who flew with Thach and named the Thach Weave maneuver after him. Great guy indeed and we had great discussions. Then of all the damned things, Ben Finney also showed up on the island and we caught up with each other. He had read about me in the newspapers and said, "You're a famous son of a bitch back home, so get ready." Finney introduced me to the actor Robert Montgomery, whom he knew well, who was also on the island. Hell, who didn't he know?

Montgomery was serving as a naval officer. You will find that the vast majority of our celebrities served in the war, and many veterans later became actors. You never saw that patriotism during Vietnam, never. But you sure as shit saw Hanoi Jane [Jane Fonda] and the antiwar, anti-American crowd. She should have been given the Tokyo Rose treatment, but her dad kept that shit from happening. Some of my friends are Jim Stockdale [Admiral James B. Stockdale] and Bud Day [Colonel George E. Day]. Both also have the Medal of Honor. Ask them their opinions sometime. Just make sure Sybil is out of the room. [*Sybil Elizabeth Stockdale (née Bailey; November 25, 1924–October 10, 2015) was a campaigner for families of Americans missing in Southeast Asia and the founder and first national coordinator of the National League of Families of American Prisoners and Missing in Southeast Asia. She was adamantly opposed to profanity, which was sure to be plentiful at the mention of Hanoi Jane.*]

Then guess who else arrived, fresh from China and Burma. Damned Boyington landed, taking over VMF-214, which was made up of replacement pilots like most of the other patchwork units. He would rack up a lot of kills, but his official score was always in dispute. I have spoken with the Marine Corps and the American Fighter Aces Association, even historians and guys who flew with Boyington in the AVG. I know Tex Hill and some of the other Flying Tigers. I know that you [Heaton] spoke with Tex, and I am sure he gave you a wealth of information on Boyington. [*Foss was correct.*]

He [Boyington] was something of a legend even back then, and I do not mean in a good way. Boyington claimed six kills with the AVG, but the guys I spoke with say he had no more than four—some say that three at most were confirmed. But his claims were accepted by the Marine Corps, so they listed him as top ace. That really does not matter to me. What gets my goat is the fact that he flaunts it, and half the time he's drunk.

I was gathering my stuff and organizing the departure for me and my men when I met a certain Lieutenant Richard M. Nixon. Yes, that one. He took care of everything—he was one squared-away swabby, but I never called him that. He was later the president, after all. He knew who I was and bent over backwards to help us out. Later when he ran for office, then the presidency, we got together a few times. With his help we were all set up and finally on the slow-as-hell transport ship back to the States. I had a lot of time to think, to remember. All the friends I had lost came back to me. I felt quite depressed, to be honest. When they died or were missing, I had to write the letters to their loved ones. That is a gut-wrenching job, worse than funeral duty, in my opinion.

Then the malaria came back with a vengeance. I thought I was going to die, but I lived, and I am still here. We docked at Long Beach [on April 19, 1943], and I was about to go to Camp Kearny when my bags were stolen. I had orders to board a C-46 for Washington, but I only had the uniform I had been wearing for a while. When I landed, I was introduced to Secretary [of the Navy Frank] Knox, Admiral [Ernest J.] King [chief of naval operations], Admiral John McCain [vice chief of naval operations and grandfather of Senator John McCain], and General Robert Denig, who was Marine Corps public relations.

They sent me everywhere and [my wife] June arrived to be

with me. That, sleeping in a real bed, and having the best of food was like heaven. Then I went on a dog-and-pony tour talking at Quantico, Annapolis, you name it. I was given a tour of the Grumman factory and addressed the people who built the Wildcat and thanked them. One stop was back home in Sioux Falls, where my mom and family met us, and the entire county showed up. Mom and I did a radio broadcast interview that went nationwide. They gave me a massive parade, and I remember thinking that I really wished my dad was there to see it.

When I was in Chicago, I connected with Roger Haberman and was glad to see he was doing well. Then I was told that I would be going back to Washington to meet President [Franklin D.] Roosevelt, and Mom and June joined me. When we walked in, Roosevelt was sitting behind the desk in his wheelchair, and he whipped out the citation and read it. Then he put the medal around my neck. Again, I thought of my dad. Well, after that, I made the cover of *Life* magazine and continued the tour. In New York I had to give a speech to I don't know how many thousands of people in Central Park. Mayor [Fiorello] La Guardia introduced me. I gave a lot of speeches, but it was all for the war effort.

After that, I was reassigned to the Goleta Marine Base at Santa Barbara, California, to train pilots. We had a good time there, and my position gave me a lot of latitude. I was creating the new VMF-115 and I chose Greg Loesch as my executive officer, and Bill Freeman as my engineering officer. I even pulled Haberman in along with others, and I could not have made better choices. The training unit was issued with the new Chance Vought F4U Corsair to replace the Wildcat, but we had serious mechanical issues. We lost a few aircraft and some pilots were killed in training. One of the bright spots was when Walt Disney personally created our unit emblem. My old unit had been the "Flying Circus," so this new one became "Joe's Jokers." The guys loved it.

My CO was Colonel Sandy Lawson, one of those pilots who was in Sioux Falls when I was a kid. He listened [to me], and then called General Bill Wallace, who knew me from Guadalcanal and who was commanding Marine Aviation West Coast at San Diego. Lawson handed me the phone, I stated my problem, and the general said I would have a technical expert the next day. I was stunned, because nothing good ever happens that fast in the Marine Corps. Courts-martial perhaps, but no great things.

Well, true to his word, I had an expert. That was when I met Charles A. Lindbergh, my childhood hero, who I had tried, but was unable, to see when he visited back home. I was stunned. This was like sending the Pope to give battlefield communion. I had him stay with June and me at the house that we rented, owned by actor Ronald Colman. Well, he figured out all the bugs in the Corsair, mostly electrical from the wiring harness suffering from vibrations affecting the contact points, and then we were cooking with gas. By the time he left, he had made a lot of friends. His recommendations on the Corsair went far up the chain and were addressed on the assembly line.

There were breaks from the maelstrom, and I made it a point to make personal visits to the families of the men I lost, the same people who received my letters. It was tough, worse than funeral duty, but I felt it was necessary. Wives and mothers were bad enough, but the kids ripped my heart out. I remember thinking that I was glad that I did not die and leave a child behind as so many did.

Well, I wanted back in the war, and we got our wish. [*Foss continuously petitioned to higher authorities to get back into action.*] After arriving on Guadalcanal, we flew to Bougainville, where the Japs were trying to take the airfield at Torokina. When we landed these new Corsairs, we had to avoid falling enemy artillery rounds as well as the big holes they made on the airstrip. Our orders were to take the worn-out old Corsairs to Guadalcanal to refuel, and then on to Espiritu Santo. One of my pilots, Lieutenant Steve Warren, volunteered to take it the rest of the way. He took off, and the damned engine blew up right over the runway. He inverted and safely bailed out. I saw the whole thing, and Steve and I still talk about that day. We did a few shuttle missions rotating aircraft. Then, while stationed on Bougainville, we got some bombing missions to hit Rabaul, New Britain, and other islands.

Well, here is a story for you. Our intelligence officer was one Joseph [R.] McCarthy. Yes, that one. Anyway, he had an idea to change the mission schedules because we were working on a set schedule, which meant the Jap AA [antiaircraft] gunners would be ready for us. The commanding general was not impressed with McCarthy's suggestion. Well, Joe McCarthy volunteered to ride backseat in some SBDs, doing thirty missions, as I recall. At least he was taking the risk with everyone else. We laughed when he said he was running for the U.S. Senate after the war. Well, in 1946 he won.

We flew a lot more bombing and strafing missions, and when we were placed on Emirau Island, we started hitting New Ireland. Emirau was an entirely different world, with game and fish. I had brought some long guns with me from the States, and we had plenty to eat. We did some night missions, looking for ships or floatplanes, truck lights on roads, anything we could shoot up, but no dogfighting. I almost bought it on my first night of strafing missions when I fired at some trucks and the muzzle flashes of my six fifties blinded me. I managed to pull up before I pancaked, but we did lose a pilot that night, probably from the same issue. Regardless, ground and sea attack missions were the order of the day. The Corsair was a natural dive-bomber more than a pure fighter aircraft anyway.

Then one day Charles Lindbergh arrived, looking for me. He wanted to fly with us, and he did so, flying the most dangerous missions for a month. He taught us a lot of valuable tricks, like extending our fuel range by adjusting the throttle and mixture, which paid heavy dividends and probably saved lives. He was extremely brave in these attacks, foolishly so on occasion. Once when we came back from a bomb run, a photographer took our picture together and it ended up in *Parade* magazine. When he had to leave, we had a good farewell with the men.

Soon after we were getting orders for New Guinea related to the planning for the Philippines.

I arrived and who the hell did I see? You betcha, Charlie Lindbergh. He was flying combat with a P-38 squadron, and actually got a kill when they were jumped. Well, the victory and AAR [after-action report] listed all participants. When MacArthur received it, he sent Lindbergh home, as it was in violation of international law for civilians to be in combat units. That was a shame. His age was also one of the issues they used against him. During the same period, my malaria was back so bad, I could hardly stand, so they ordered me home for good. My war was effectively over. I spent six months under the care of an infectious-disease specialist in Klamath Falls, Oregon, and was never bothered by malaria again.

Upon my departure, my new assignment was commander of the Marine base right there in Klamath Falls. This was grunt duty, not flying. Colonel George Van Orden was the base CO and a famous sniper and infantry shooting expert. We went duck hunting a lot. That was good duty. I was invited to fly to a ranch at Lakeview to hunt once by the governor [Earl Wilcox Snell] and [the president of the state senate Marshall Coronet], and their pilot [Cliff Hogue], so I went once, but never again. I did not like their flying and landing methods, so I always found a reason to not go. Later all three were killed when they crashed. I just had a feeling.

Then I found out that FDR had died. [Harry S.] Truman became president and then Germany surrendered. I knew the Pacific War would go on for a while longer. The day after Japan surrendered, I was sent to Washington to discuss my remaining on active duty. When I stated that I had requested a regular commission, I was told that Secretary Knox had approved it back in 1943. It just never made it down the chain of command, not even to Geiger. But I had decided to go civilian anyway, and I separated.

After bouncing around with my childhood friend Duke Corning for a long time, I went back to flying with a Marine reserve unit out of Minneapolis, and then Duke and I decided to start our own flying service. He joined the Navy and flew B-24 Liberators with Joseph Kennedy Jr. over Europe, and later flew Corsair night fighters. He was well qualified. When we went to the bank manager and told him we wanted $75,000, he looked like he was going to have a stroke. We had no collateral. Well, we left thinking about our next move. The next day the phone rang, and it was the bank manager. We had our money!

I was broke. My first daughter, Cheryl, was born with cerebral palsy, and June had her own health issues, diabetes being one of them. I paid for medical treatments out of pocket and we struggled for a couple of years after I got out of the service. There were other problems also. The airplane business burned down, but we got it back and running. President Truman wanted to cut the defense budget, which would have dangerously reduced the flying hours for pilots to remain current. I went to see the secretary of defense, Louis Johnson, had a discussion about that, and settled the issue. Later, back home, I was talked into going into politics.

Well, we started Foss's Flying Service while I was still flying Corsairs with the reserves, maintaining air time. Our business grew and we acquired more planes. We taught flying and flew people around, good work when you can get it. Then one day [Brigadier] General Ted Arndt showed up and told me that South Dakota was going to have its own Air National Guard unit, attached to the Air Force. I was offered the job of leading it and choosing my own people. I resigned from the Marine Reserves and became a lieutenant colonel in the stepchild of the Air Force. Of course, Duke went with me. I retired from there as a brigadier general. During that time, we also started a car dealership, and business was good. We had a couple of floods and a fire that ruined the flying business, but we always bounced back.

I ran and won a seat in the state legislature, but June was never enthusiastic about my career in politics. I guess I am most proud of the Crippled Children's Hospital and School in Sioux Falls. It meant a lot to me because of Cheryl and other children like her. In 1954, I was president of the South Dakota Society for Crippled Children and Adults, and years later, I became the national president.

I always believed that we needed to care for all Americans. My position in Pierre, South Dakota, [at the Society for Crippled Children] made all of that possible, but in 1949 I decided to run for governor. I lost in a three-way primary, which I would have won, had it only been two of us. I am certain of this because I was only a couple of thousand votes shy of winning. But

I was reelected to the state house, and in 1954 I ran for governor again and cleaned up in the primary. The general election was basically a landslide. At thirty-nine, I was the youngest governor in South Dakota's history. My mom was with me when I took the oath, and I thought about my dad again and how he would be proud—that I turned out to be a Republican at least, if nothing else.

I was still a colonel when Korea broke out. I wanted to go, but was told no in very clear terms due to the Medal of Honor. The government felt that it would be bad PR if I were killed or captured. I went to Washington to speak with General [Hoyt] Vandenberg, who also flatly said no. I ran into Senator Francis Case, from my state, and I told him in strict confidence why I was in Washington. Then I saw a newspaper with my picture that stated I wanted to go fight in Korea. Well, "depressed" is a word I could use.

It was not all bad because I started flying in the Air Force the next year and my son Frank was born [August 9, 1951]. June was working at the hospital when polio broke out, and our son contracted it. She felt responsible, having been in contact with children who had it. But he recovered, and for that, I thanked God.

I guess I was blessed in many ways. I held many positions, but governor was my favorite job outside the military, as far as public service was concerned. At first, I had a strained relationship with [Dwight D.] Eisenhower when he was president, but I turned that around, and Nixon always liked me. He remembered those days during the war with fondness. I refused to run for a third term as governor, because I felt that term limits were critical, but I did run for the House of Representatives and lost to George McGovern.

Later I was offered many different civilian jobs. Even Eddie Rickenbacker offered me a position at Eastern Airlines, but his business management method did not suit me. It was the same with other companies, but I did work for Raven Industries for a while. Then I was asked to be the commissioner of the American Football League that was newly formed to rival the NFL. That was in 1959, a long time ago. I loved the job, but it killed my marriage with June. She had had enough. The one bright spot was that I was able to fly various military aircraft, keeping up my hours as I was still in the Guard.

Ironically, during all the transition work into jets for the Air Force, I had met my second wife, Donna, while in Arizona. She had been divorced for some time, and had a daughter, Coni, and a son, Dean. I had the occasion to run into her whenever I was at Williams Air Force Base. A decade later, while I was still separated pending the divorce, I ran into her again in Colorado, where I'd gone for an AFA [Air Force Association] reunion. Later on, I would become president of the AFA—go figure—and a Marine as well.

During my various careers and experiences, I made a lot of celebrity friends. On that note, I think I even caught up with Ben Finney. It was good to have friends like that who were real, genuine people in real life. Bing Crosby was one, and so were

Danny Thomas and others like Gary Cooper. Bob Hope was the best and he served our nation well through several wars, entertaining our servicemen overseas. President John F. Kennedy was a special relationship, and we were friends despite our political differences. He was a nice man, and we had a lot in common, like football and hunting. Plus, he was as famous, or even more famous, for his wartime experience as I was, and rightly so. Danny Thomas was one of the best people who ever lived, and I still support St. Jude Children's [Research] Hospital. Every year that I can make it, I attend the Medal of Honor reunions. All the living recipients who can make it come together, and that is usually where we see each other. Those are always lively.

Well, I always try to stay busy. Later in life, I traveled the world, and I have been on safaris in Africa, India, and everywhere—such as nice hunting trips in the Rocky Mountains with my wife, Didi [Donna], and friends. I hung out with a couple of guys you [Heaton] also know, Curtis LeMay and Jimmy Doolittle, and I hunted with Roy Rogers, Robert Stack, John Wayne, Robert Taylor, and a lot of guys who were avid outdoorsmen. Perhaps one of my best friends was Charlton Heston, a great American, and we were both high rollers in the National Rifle Association. Since I was twice governor of South Dakota, I later considered running for the U.S. Senate again in Washington, but changed my mind.

And I had a couple of outdoor television shows like *The American Sportsman* that I really enjoyed doing. Our first show was in Kenya, with Robert Stack as the first celebrity guest. He shot and killed a rogue lion that was killing Masai cattle and was welcomed as a hero. We got that on film, too! During that trip I killed a rogue elephant that was raiding a small village. That footage became famous and was the clip that introduced the series. We also did fishing and bird hunting for the shows. That was a great time, and I got paid to do it. The first season's ratings were so good, we filmed a second in India, hunting a tiger. We had a third and final season, because the writers were doing things I disagreed with. No matter how good the money, if I was morally opposed to something, I walked away. I thought about my dad again and what he would do. I did the right thing.

But then another door opened, and I did a series called *The Outdoorsman: Joe Foss*. I liked the idea. I also brought Didi into it as a still photographer, since she had the talent for it. We even involved the kids, making it a family type of show. Again, we traveled the world, mostly North America. I got arsenic poisoning in a cornfield that had been sprayed. It was bad, but I survived. In 1967, we decided to get married after several years together, so we went to Hawaii. We continued our trips to Africa and we dined with Queen Elizabeth in Scotland and Didi bagged a nice stag.

Well, my days as commissioner of the American Football League were coming to an end, which was OK with me. I really pissed off all the right people when I moved the big game from New Orleans to Houston because of the racism my black players were experiencing. I never tolerated that bigoted racist shit, and I was about to make that city pay for it by costing them revenue. When that became public, it was a national scandal. "Screw them," I said. After the TV shows ended, I went to work for KLM [Airlines]. It was interesting representing them in Washington. Then I had a scare with a bout of pericarditis, which sidelined me for a couple of months.

I have met every president from Roosevelt onward, and I will say this about Jimmy Carter's staff. They disappointed me when they said he was too busy to honor a request from some Dutch World War II veterans. These people had been in the underground, rescuing American airmen who were shot down. That was plain bad and disrespectful. Carter later amended that staff decision and met with them. He should have fired those people. I would have. I would say the one president I had the most in common with was Ronald Reagan, who was a great man and a friend. We always saw eye to eye.

I attend the Medal of Honor reunions when I can. One year, Boyington was there, drunk as usual, and wanting to fight with someone. He locked eyes with me, yelled, "Foss, I'm coming!" and charged at me, pinning me to the wall. He was very strong and outweighed me, he being a shorter, stocky bastard. He wanted to wrestle, but I was having none of it. The word had spread about Boyington's questionable victory record, but even worse, about his conduct as a prisoner of war. Many of the others just avoided him to be polite. However, there were a couple who did not mind taking him down a peg or two, and there were some serious heated arguments. I will leave it at that, no reason to air dirty laundry. Let's just say of all the recipients,

Boyington was the least welcomed. If I had to sum up what I think it means to be an American, I would say this. Be a good citizen; be true to yourself and others. Honor your country and God and take care of your family. If your country calls for you, it is because it needs you, so accept that call. It is your duty to help protect what we all fought for throughout our history. We owe it to those who fought before us. Every generation sets the standard for those that follow. And we damned sure owe it to the generations who will follow. We are the protectors of freedom, and that is not a duty that can be taken lightly.

MEDAL OF HONOR CITATION

Capt. Joseph J. Foss, USMC

For outstanding heroism and courage above and beyond the call of duty as Executive Officer of a Marine Fighting Squadron, at Guadalcanal, Solomon Islands. Engaging in almost daily combat with the enemy from October 9 to November 19, 1942, Capt. Foss personally shot down 23 Japanese aircraft and damaged others so severely that their destruction was extremely probable. In addition, during this period, he successfully led a large number of escort missions, skillfully covering reconnaissance, bombing and photographic planes as well as surface craft. On January 15, 1943, he added three more enemy aircraft to his already brilliant successes for a record of aerial combat achievement unsurpassed in this war. Boldly searching out an approaching enemy force on January 25, Capt. Foss led his eight F4F Marine planes and four Army P-38s into action and, undaunted by tremendously superior numbers, intercepted and struck with such force that four Japanese fighters were shot down and the bombers were turned back without releasing a single bomb. His remarkable flying skill, inspiring leadership and indomitable fighting spirit were distinctive factors in the defense of strategic American positions on Guadalcanal.

Franklin D. Roosevelt, May 18, 1943

CAPTAIN DAVID McCAMPBELL, USN (RET.)

JANUARY 16, 1910–JUNE 30, 1996

The story of David McCampbell, another American who rose to the occasion during World War II, resembles in many respects the early life of other famous pilots of his day who came from humble beginnings. His education followed a rather unusual path, but he managed to graduate from Annapolis, and eventually received his commission in 1934. Despite having been a naval officer for several years before the United States became involved in the war, he was late getting into combat.

When he did arrive in the Pacific, he took off and made up for lost time: in his first seven months of service, McCampbell destroyed thirty-four enemy planes in aerial combat, the greatest number of enemy planes that an American pilot ever shot down during a single tour of combat duty. This included nine in one mission, another record for an American pilot; on this same mission, he also destroyed well over twenty planes on the ground and assisted in sinking several Japanese ships. This first, incredible tour of duty made McCampbell the top-scoring naval fighter pilot of World War II. The most highly decorated naval aviator of World War II, he received the Medal of Honor, Navy Cross, Silver Star, Legion of Merit, and Distinguished Flying Cross, among many other honors and awards.

Despite his skill as a combat fighter pilot, McCampbell always stressed "team effort," communication, and situational awareness. While he personally acknowledged his own skill and success, he believed that the best missions were the ones when all of his men came home: losing a pilot or crewman was too hard to take. Deservedly enshrined in the National Aviation Hall of Fame, David McCampbell was also one all-around great human being.

The late historian, author, and pilot Jeffrey L. Ethell introduced me to McCampbell in 1989. After a long series of telephone discussions, I was finally able to meet him in 1994 at his home in West Palm Beach, Florida. I came prepared with a plethora of notes from our many phone calls and plenty of background research, thanks to the help of Jeff, who generously offered me unlimited access to his extensive library whenever I visited him in Front Royal, Virginia.

I found McCampbell very cordial and highly intelligent. Like

Foss, he was down-to-earth and matter-of-fact. Unlike Boyington, he did not embellish his achievements. He spoke of his life and career as if they were just facts, never overstating. His humility was such that I sometimes had to pose a question several times to get him to fill in the details.

After our interview, McCampbell had an accident in August 1994 and apparently broke his hip. Following a period of illness, he passed away on June 30, 1996. I learned of his death from Jeff, who called to tell me that David had "gone west." Ironically, a year later almost to the day, Jeff, too, "went west." On June 6, 1997, I received a call from my friend and fellow historian Jon Guttman, telling me that Jeff had just died flying a P-38 Lightning at an air show in Oregon. His family had been in attendance. That hit hard.

For me personally, the 1990s were a decade of loss when Jeff and many of the gifted pilots I had interviewed over the years passed away. Jeff was a good friend who had helped get me my start as I set out to interview some of the greatest pilots the world has ever known. I will ever be grateful to him and the historian Colonel Raymond F. Toliver, my friends and mentors, for the invaluable aid they gave me at the start of my career. Fortunately, my relationships with Ethell and Toliver, as well as those with others, were the reasons for my even having contact with these great pilots such as David McCampbell, and McCampbell considered them good friends.

DAVID McCAMPBELL

I was born on January 16, 1910, in Bessemer, Alabama. I grew up on a small farm, milking cows, collecting eggs from the chickens, and living a very rural type of life until we moved to Florida. I was about twelve, I think, when we relocated, and my dad opened a furniture and appliance store. I know a lot of pilots—like Joe Foss and some others—always dreamed of flying when they were boys, but that was not really in my head until I went up in a Jenny. Aviation only really became a thing because of the First World War. We all heard about Eddie Rickenbacker, Frank Luke, and those guys, as well as the Germans like [Manfred von] Richthofen, [Ernst] Udet, and the British and French pilots. I recall reading about guys like Mick Mannock and René Fonck.

I enjoyed sports and was good at swimming and baseball, and I played football in school. I was competitive, which I think is a character trait inherent to good fighter pilots. When I looked at my men, I could always tell who were the most aggressive. I liked that in a pilot, but it had to be tempered with good judgment. I had a pretty solid education compared to most boys like me from the Deep South. I could read well and loved Western books and things like that.

Life was good for a long time. It was a slower pace of living than what we have today. Not everybody had a car and there were few highways—hell, we did not even have that many paved roads. But I remember my dad became really upset after the stock market problems in [October] 1929. Suddenly, everyone was out of work. People could not afford to buy basic necessities, and the things my dad sold suddenly became luxury items that no one wanted or could afford. Most people spent the next decade just trying to survive. If you had land and livestock, where you could grow food and have meat and eggs, you had a much better life than people living in cities, who were looking for jobs that were simply not available.

If I had to guess, I would say that the experience of growing up and living during that time made us more self-reliant and determined as a people. When you have to fight every day to feed a family or pay a mortgage, it toughens you up, so by the time we entered the war, we were already pretty pissed off as a nation. The Japs just pulled the trigger. About a year after we moved to Florida, I managed to attend the Staunton Military Academy in Virginia just before I started high school. That was a good experience. It was a private boarding school, but my dad somehow made the money for the tuition. The school had a ROTC program, kind of a juvenile West Point. We had military discipline, inspections, calisthenics, a lot of history, geography, mathematics, languages, science, literature—the full curriculum. It was a very good prep school for those looking at military academies such as West Point or the Naval Academy. We learned to march and salute, and had daily PT and even marksmanship instruction. The academics were more rigorous than I expected, but I managed to graduate after a delay due to illness. There was hazing, but that was no big deal to me, just part of the program. It toughened me up in other ways.

Barry Goldwater was one of the fellas there with me. We had a lot in common and were both in the ROTC program. His family owned a department store, furniture and things like that, as did my dad. We both played baseball and football and swam. Barry was very competitive and good at all sports. I was always a good swimmer, and I then started diving, which I was also good at. Now, Barry, he was always a real A-type personality. He was not afraid to stand up for something if he really believed it was right. That is a trait I admire in anyone. He and I also had the same [negative] opinion about segregation, especially in the military. I did not see any reason for it. I saw the discrimination as a boy for sure, but nothing so overt as to worry about at the time.

But Goldwater was a fanatic about it. After the war, he used the example of General Benjamin [O.] Davis [the first African American general in the Air Force] to dispel the myths that supported continued segregation. He was just not on board with that type of thinking. We had many discussions about that very subject and he never bought into Lyndon Johnson's emergence as a great advocate for blacks. He ran against Johnson in the 1964 presidential election and lost huge, but he knew that old LBJ had pretty much bribed his way into the presidency.

Barry went to college at the University of Arizona and then

into the Army Air Corps, later called the Army Air Force, and then just the Air Force when it became a separate branch of the military. He was also a pilot and a Republican senator for a number of years. He had great stories to tell about his time during the war, and he later was a driving force in getting the Air Force recognized as a separate branch of service and pushing for the creation of the Air Force Academy. He retired as a major general.

Prior to graduation, I had to think about what college I wanted to go to. The University of Alabama was my primary choice, but that did not work out, so I was accepted into the Georgia Institute of Technology in Atlanta, where I planned on studying civil engineering. My father's family had a construction business back in Alabama, and as far as I know, they did not suffer as a result of the Depression. People still needed buildings, roads, and things like that.

I was a good math student, which is a real bonus for an engineer, and I decided to play football. Being a freshman on the junior team, I looked at the huge monsters on the varsity team, who we were to play against. I was a buck sixty, and the concept of self-preservation kicked in. I decided that getting seriously injured was not the best course of action, so I focused on my studies. I had a great time there since I had a car, which most of the guys did not. I was on the swim team and continued my diving.

I had always liked ships and had read all about them, so I joined the NROTC [Naval Reserve Officers Training Program], which helped prepare me for acceptance to Annapolis. After I did the summer cruise on the [USS] *New York*, which was a battleship, I thought about going to the Naval Academy. Going to college was expensive, and I knew that the service academies were free with a commitment. I had no problem with that but getting accepted to the academies was not an easy process.

An applicant had to get nominated by someone in the federal government, like a congressman or senator. Then you had to pass the entrance exam, which I did, but not with great scores. My math skills were superb, but the English and grammar portion was my Achilles' heel. I was never a good writer, although I read a lot of books. It was like Spanish; I just did not take to it. Well, I finally got on the list behind some other guy, but he failed to qualify. Being the next in line, I was given the appointment.

Now I was in a very different environment, but I was well suited to it. The hazing was expected, as we incoming plebes were always harassed by the upperclassmen. They gave us nicknames. Mine was "Soupy," but I have no idea why they chose that. It was just one of the things you endured. I was one of the midshipmen who collected the least demerits—black marks against you for doing something that violates good order and discipline. You could get demerits for almost anything, such as getting out of bed late, being late to the mess hall, silly things most often, but they added up. If you received too many, they would convene a board and could expel you. I made sure that did not happen. I earned my demerits honestly but infrequently.

Well, I always liked sports, so I made the swim team and the dive team. These were areas where I could stand out in a good way. We competed against all the Ivy League schools and others. I really enjoyed it and became the Atlantic Coast diving champion as well as the Eastern Intercollegiate champion. I thought about maybe trying out for the Olympic team, but I was still suffering with low grades in my Spanish courses. That shit plagued me. I also wanted to play baseball, but that did not work out, either.

Not all of academy life was hazing and suffering. We did have a social life, such as it was—chaperoned events, dances, things like that. There I met a girl I had known in Florida, Sally-Jane. Later we got married; it was my second go-around. I managed to do another cruise and went to Europe aboard the battleship *Alabama*. We all took turns pulling duty, various watches and such. We hit Scotland, France, Germany. I was able to travel and see Edinburgh and Paris, and took time off to see Hamburg after we docked in Kiel. I really enjoyed that tour and learned a lot.

When we docked stateside, it was back to the academic grind. We also heard that only about half the class would receive commissions because Congress had limited them. I was definitely not in the top half academically, so I felt pretty sure I would have a degree but no career in the Navy.

My next cruise was on the battleship *Florida*. I thought it was ironic and strange that my cruises were on two ships named for the states I had lived in. This cruise took us into the Gulf of Mexico to Houston and the Caribbean, where we hit Puerto

Rico, Bermuda, and Cuba. I always enjoyed cruises, and I knew that I wanted to be a career officer. I also worked on my Morse code rating, as that was critical in the naval service, and became quite good at transmitting and translating incoming codes. I was also once again thinking about the flying option.

One thing that really grabbed my interest at the academy was my introduction to aviation, where I was able to ride in some twin-engine aircraft, seaplanes. I really took to it and began learning all I could about flying. As I pursued that interest later, my math skills really paid off, especially for instrument navigation. That is a critical skill when you are flying over great regions of ocean without any landmarks to use as a visual reference. When you are totally on instruments, that compass and clock become your best friends, believe me.

I graduated in 1933 with a degree in Marine Engineering and looked forward to being commissioned in the regular Navy, but since Congress had placed limits on the number of officers in all branches of the military, I was basically discharged from the regular Navy and later commissioned as an ensign in the Naval Reserves. That was not a steady paycheck. I was not sure what I would be able to do about flight school, because regular commissioned officers got first shot at those billets, so I went back home. I worked in the family business for a while, doing construction work, short-term jobs. I then worked at the local hardware store but was still not making much money.

I heard that there were jobs in California, Washington, and Oregon. Most were in the logging industry, something I knew absolutely nothing about, but I would see what happened. When I failed to get basic work, I walked into the Douglas Aircraft Company and applied. I was hired and worked as a mechanic and sheet metal riveter working on DC-2 and DC-3 transport aircraft and on the assembly line for a few months. The pay was better, and it was good work. You have to remember that the Great Depression had really hit the country hard. It was not over, and I felt lucky to at least have a job. The experience of seeing how planes were built was logged into my head.

Ray Thompson, one of my classmates from the Annapolis swim team, was there [in Santa Monica]. He had made the Olympic swim team and was there with the actor Buster Crabbe, the original Flash Gordon in the films. I met him and his wife through Ray, and we became friends. That was great, because I was invited to swim and do some diving at the very prestigious Hollywood Athletic Club. This was where Johnny Weissmuller, who played Tarzan, and other big-time celebrities of the day went to play tennis, swim, or just hang out at the lounge.

I always kept my eye on what was going on in the world and kept on applying for a regular commission. In 1934 it was granted, and I was transferred from the reserves to the active-duty Navy. I felt lucky and I was looking forward to going to sea, but the thought of flying was still present. I was very pleased and drove from Santa Monica back to West Palm Beach to visit Mom and Dad. When I reported, I was assigned to the [USS] *Portland*, which was a heavy cruiser. They assigned me to the electrical division, handling what you would expect: all aspects of a ship's electrical power, communications to include shipboard radios and lights—you name it. That division had some really sharp sailors in it and the job was not a problem.

As the new ensign, I stood a lot of watch, and I expected that. I also pulled a lot of engine watch and became really familiar with the workings of a ship's engine room. The ship had four engines, big bastards, like all big warships. When they kick on, there is a loud, throaty hum that you can hear belowdecks. There is really nothing like it. The only thing more impressive was when the eight-inch guns fired, which was rare.

I had additional duties, such as assistant gunnery officer for the five-inch guns. I was also made catapult officer, because we had a seaplane, a Curtiss Seagull, on the aft, which was launched by a steam catapult. This was a two-seat floatplane, pilot and rear gunner. It was a biplane used for scouting, but also had the ability to carry small bombs. I always loved watching the operation as it was pulled along the rails and fired like a slingshot over the ocean. I thought that must be a great feeling. On return, it landed in the water and was retrieved by a crane. I became more determined than ever to change my course and applied for flight school. This was not just for the adventure, but because the flight pay was better.

My time came when I was able to fly as the observer in the scout plane, which dovetailed with my duties as the aerial gunnery observer. My capability to use Morse code now paid off. You have to remember, our aircraft did not have widespread verbal radio communications gear at the time, although those were coming online. Being skilled at Morse code was a bonus in case you lost radio contact or had to use a signal mirror, should you go down and need to contact someone for rescue. Luckily, I never had to go that far. I would be responsible for giving corrections to the shipboard guns, watching the impact of shells during firing operations. We were also the eyes and technical ears when it came to locating enemies in time of war.

We were once on a training flight with another Seagull and it went down. The visibility was shit due to heavy fog, but we managed to locate the plane, circling as I relayed the position. We stayed on station too long to make it back to the *Portland*, so we landed and were picked up by the *Chicago*, and the *Portland* collected the other crew. I still wanted to fly. Besides, I was always looking to do new things. The extra pay would come in handy when I married my girlfriend Susan in 1936, after a couple of years on the *Portland*.

We had been throughout the Pacific and had even hit Midway Island, which would become famous, as you know. We carried Marines who did beach-landing exercises. That was interesting—it made me glad I was not a Marine. Then we headed back home to Long Beach. The *Portland* was a busy ship with a good crew.

It really got a workout when we later went through the Panama Canal into the Caribbean and into the Atlantic to New York, where our sister ship, the *Houston*, was berthed with us. We got a large party of visitors there when President [Franklin D.] Roosevelt decided to take a trip with his entourage. He and the main staff were on the *Houston*, and the rest of the show was on board the *Portland* with us. We cruised to Baja and stayed for a few days so they could do some fishing, then powered up, cruised through the Panama Canal, and took the entire group to Charleston [South Carolina]. We headed back through Panama again when we returned to the West Coast.

We had a couple of ship captains. One we all admired was a World War I hero, Captain Willis Bradley Jr. I never forgot him. He had the Medal of Honor, but he was approachable, not standoffish. He also had faith in his junior officers and gave us greater responsibilities. That earned him our loyalty and we earned his respect. That is the best relationship you can have, and believe me, it is not always the case. When we pulled into San Francisco, he gave me command of the ship to bring her in. Right there, we cruised under the Golden Gate Bridge, and I was proud as hell because I was just a junior officer.

We had been doing battle fleet exercises, a big workup—really a maritime war game—and had covered a lot of ocean from the Aleutian Islands to Hawaii and Midway. This was when we had to go to Pearl Harbor for an overhaul, which gave us some great shore leave and allowed me to get married. Susan and I married in Honolulu, Hawaii, while the ship was in port for the refit. She wanted to honeymoon in paradise, and we were going to be there for a while anyway.

After we put into port, several of us, all aspiring pilots, had to go for the eye exam. My applications for flight training seemed to have paid off. Well, shit being what it was, all of us failed the flight surgeon's eye exam! We all knew that that was bullshit, because I had had a complete physical the previous year. I was fine, eyes and all, but that "was not a flight surgeon's examination." "Bullshit," I said. I finally took another exam and passed and was approved for flight school.

I arrived for flight school at the Naval Air Station in Pensacola, Florida, where they also trained Marine Corps pilots. We trained on the standard aircraft used by the Army. Being Navy, we also trained for short takeoff and landing procedures because we knew we would have to fly from aircraft carriers. Carriers were new to the Navy—hell, they were new to warfare in general. The one thing we all learned was to be aggressive. Be the first guy to throw a punch and keep hitting until your guys are the only ones left in the air. Later, when I became a leader, that is what I instilled into my guys—total combat. Passiveness will never make a good fighter, but it can damn sure make a dead one.

As with most flight training programs, we had some accidents. A couple of guys were killed, but I personally never really had any problems. I was good at aerial gunnery and aerobatics, and I took to the trainers without any problem. Aerobatics and ability determined where you went, whether to fighters, dive-bombers, torpedo bombers, or whatever. Your flight school record and instructors' recommendations pretty much decided your fate.

Nothing made me prouder than to get those gold wings pinned on. The training had been very rigorous, but then it had to be. You had to have the best men in those cockpits. I had graduated near the top of my class, which allowed me to choose my type of assignment. Of course, I chose fighters. We all knew that there was going to be a war. Europe was all screwed up, and the civil war in Spain seemed like a real shit dance. Japan had gone nuts in Asia and was rampaging all over China. Later Hitler took Austria and then Czechoslovakia. I just waited, knowing that we were going to fight at some point. Too much had been going on in Asia and Europe for something not to happen. There was no way all of these events were not going to drag us into it.

My new orders put me on the USS *Ranger*, where I was assigned to Flying Squadron 4. We were flying the Grumman F3F, a biplane with an enclosed canopy. That was the last biplane fighter the Navy ever used because the [F4F] Wildcat was on the way. The next phase for me was carrier qualification. As I was Navy, that was a requirement. I did pretty well on my practice landings and traps but had an issue with the night landing. I failed to lower the tailhook and hit the barrier, missing the wire, but I still qualified. This was where I damaged my nose, when my head went forward on impact and my face hit the gunsight, but it was a small price to pay.

I was the new lieutenant junior grade and assigned as wingman to [Lieutenant (Junior Grade or JG)] Joe Clifton. He was a different kind of guy and had been an all-American football player in college. Flying his wing was not easy; I can tell you that. One thing I will say is that we did a lot of flying, and the many takeoffs and landings only enhanced my skill. But we also flew mock dogfights, intercepts, and practiced a lot of formation flying. We practiced mock attacks on other aircraft, working out the best angles, and although we did not fire ammunition, I wanted to practice getting in off-angle positions, deflection shots, and high-speed rolls. I knew that all of these methods would become valuable.

Soon after we had completed a lot of fleet exercises, I was rated as a top pilot and made a division leader, but that was also because I had seniority. We had a great group of pilots, and the ship was basically a good place to be. I have to say that once again the hand of irony was in play. The ship's captain was John [Sidney] McCain, Senator McCain's grandfather. He was an Annapolis man, as were all the McCains. Captain McCain was also one of the oldest Navy pilots. He had been around as long as Jesus and served in the First World War.

What makes a great ship is the morale of the crew, and under McCain morale was excellent. He was not a heavy-handed old disciplinarian who was aloof from his men. He thought nothing of stopping and asking a new seaman how he was doing or offering someone on the bridge coffee and getting it himself. He was just a genuine person, no pretense and no drama. That attitude extended into the air division also. My first CO was Lieutenant Commander Wendell G. Switzer, a good pilot who carried on that feeling of comradeship. I later had Lieutenant Commander Albert [K.] Morehouse, a different type of leader who was not as personable, but still a good leader.

I spent a couple of years on the *Ranger* before I was transferred to the *Wasp*. How this happened is sort of strange, and when I learned the details, I was not very excited about the new assignment. This was when our group was in Norfolk in April 1940, and we [the *Ranger*] sailed in June. I learned that the *Wasp* needed a new LSO [landing signal officer], as theirs had retired. Being the LSO meant I would have reduced flying time. But I also knew that the LSO was one of the most critical jobs on a ship and having a good one saved aircraft and lives. It was a great responsibility, and not one to be dismissed lightly. Men lived or died according to the job the LSO did. It was sacred duty, really.

The job of LSO consisted of standing on the flight deck on a special platform. You watched as the aircraft came into the landing pattern, what we call the glide slope, looking at the height of the aircraft from the deck, estimating his approach speed and his horizontal attitude. You had a paddle in each hand that allowed you to signal the pilot, and you mirrored each other. The pilot made his corrections based upon what the LSO did. If the LSO was not satisfied with the approach for any reason, he would wave off the pilot for a go-around. This told the pilot to give power, fly past, and come around again.

If all was good as the plane crossed the threshold at the fantail, the LSO then motioned for the pilot to cut power and touch down to allow the tailhook to snag the arresting wire, stopping the forward momentum of the aircraft. If the first wire did not catch, there was a second one, but if no wires were caught, a barrier stopped the aircraft from continuing forward. The stop was often quite abrupt, and many pilots in their early qualifications banged their heads against instrument panels, I can tell you. The LSO's only communication was visual. He had no radio contact with the pilot, although as we later obtained radios in the fighters, the pilot did have radio communications with the ship.

I managed to continue flying some and did carrier-landing certifications as we headed to the Caribbean Sea en route to Cuba with a destroyer escort [USS *Morris*]. During this time, we had a plane go down, and although both ships rushed to the scene, the plane, pilot, and gunner were never recovered. [*This was a SB2U-2 Vindicator, which was the U.S. Navy's first monoplane scout/dive-bomber and was second only to the TBD-1 Devastator as an operational carrier-based monoplane of any type for the Navy.*] We did more carrier qualifications, and were joined at Norfolk by the 1st Marine Air Wing, who were doing their carrier qualifications on the *Wasp*. When we left Norfolk, we went on to Boston Navy Yard, where we gave a twenty-one-gun salute as Roosevelt's yacht came into view.

We had to go back to sea for more trials and so we left for Norfolk again. I believe we picked up VF-7s and VS-72s while they did their qualifications, and continued sea trials until we reached Norfolk, where the ship had some maintenance work. This was in September, I think. After that, things got somewhat interesting, because we loaded up a squadron of Army P-40s. [*These were twenty-four Curtiss Warhawks from the*

8th Pursuit Squadron and some nine Army observation planes. These were North American O-47A reconnaissance and observation aircraft.]

This was a test to see how non-carrier-based aircraft would do taking off. Of course, landing would not be an option. And it was also an exercise to see how well a carrier could perform ferry duty carrying land-based aircraft. It all worked out well. As we learned later, Doolittle did that with B-25s from the USS *Hornet* to hit Tokyo in April of 1942. Once again, we sailed into Guantánamo Bay with two destroyers, the USS *Plunkett* and the USS *Niblack*, and were met by the USS *Texas* with the fleet admiral [Rear Admiral Hayne Ellis].

This was a great time for workups, and I managed to get more flying in as we continued the endless takeoffs and traps. The dive-bombers were being worked to death, and the pace was so frenetic, you just had the feeling that something was coming. Our group was solid on carrier-based operations, which we continued all through October and November of 1940. We then had orders to Norfolk, which meant we could spend Christmas back home. Shore leave for almost a month was incredible, but then we headed out again for a couple of months of exercises in Guantánamo Bay before returning to port in Norfolk.

On the way we were alerted to a distress signal, and a ship was in trouble. Our ship rescued the eight crewmen off Cape Hatteras and later put them ashore. [*This was the 152-foot lumber schooner* George E. Klinck *that sank on its way to Maine on*

March 8, 1941.] When we reached Norfolk, the ship went in for maintenance and to be fitted with a new long-range radar system for surface ship and aircraft detection. After more work-ups, we set sail again for the Caribbean, which seemed to be a favorite destination for the Navy. We liked it a lot and spent a lot of time at sea. When I was promoted to lieutenant in May of 1941, I had more responsibilities, which was fine with me. I just wanted to get more flying in. One responsibility was Francis, my first [child], born when I was married to Susan. I was married to my second wife, Sara-Jane, when David was born in 1945 and John in 1948. Dave also graduated from Annapolis and had a career in the Navy. They were all great kids.

We left the Caribbean for the North Atlantic, where our convoys were protected by American and British destroyers. [*This was a mission to escort the forty-four merchant ships of the eastbound convoy HX-156, which arrived in Liverpool, England, on November 5, 1941.*] We had previously given the British fifty old World War I–era destroyers as part of the lend-lease deal and supplied them with war matériel. We were still officially neutral in the war, but that was just a case of semantics. We were definitely involved, just not shooting at anyone. We then hit the North Atlantic, and things took on a different tone. Europe had been at war for two years, and FDR was sending war supplies to Britain and Russia. German subs were sinking a lot of the ships, many of them American merchant ships.

Our task force was rather large, with ships from Holland,

Canada, Britain, Belgium, Norway—just about all the Allied maritime nations involved. Some I should mention are the *Reuben James*, *Kearny*, and *Salinas*, which became major issues when they were hit by German subs. With the *Reuben James*, we had an American warship sunk by a belligerent party. We had great discussions about it. Some thought that it meant we were going to war against Germany and Italy, but others, who had more knowledge of the subject than I did, argued that the sinking was not an overt act of war. This was because our ships were escorting many British and neutral ships carrying war supplies in international waters, making them legitimate targets.

[*USS* Kearny *was hit by* U-568, *commanded by* Kapitänleutnant *Joachim Preuss at 0417 hours on October 17, 1941. Kearny* lost 11 *men out of 199 crewmen and was severely damaged but did not sink and was later repaired. The fleet oiler USS* Salinas *was struck but not sunk by* U-106, *commanded by* Kapitänleutnant *Jürgen Oesten. The USS* Reuben James *was sunk at approximately 0543 hours on October 31, 1941, by* U-552, *commanded by* Kapitänleutnant *Erich Topp. The* Reuben James *was the only ship sunk as a result of the German attacks and was the first American warship sunk by hostile action. A total of thirty-six men were rescued by the USS* Niblack.]

Following these losses, we received orders to respond if we encountered any German vessels engaging the convoys. This was just short of a declaration of war. I had been on the *Wasp* almost two years when the war broke out. I can tell you that the escort duty raised the awareness level. Torpedoes were not smart bombs, and any ship could be hit. We still had a lot of threats out there because of all the countries involved. We talked about the ships that were hit and the lives lost. There was no doubt that when we finally got into the war, there would be a lot more loss of life.

We were in Bermuda, just off the escort duty, when we heard about the attack on Pearl Harbor and Roosevelt's address to the nation. I knew right then that it was game on. We pulled into Norfolk just before Christmas since the *Wasp* needed work done. In January we were out again, and during a shakedown scenario, the *Wasp* collided with a destroyer [USS *Stack* on March 17, 1942], causing a lot of damage. *Wasp* was not damaged, believe it or not, and the destroyer managed to go in for repairs. That was one of those moments where you are awakened by the alarms, wondering what the hell is going on. I know that it was bad visibility, but that destroyer skipper's career had to be in serious question. That would be worse than running aground, really.

Right after that, we were sent back to Norfolk to be resupplied and then went to Scotland. Since we were now officially at war with Germany, Italy, and Japan, there was no reason to be coy about our missions. We sent our dive-bombers ashore and then loaded up some forty-odd Royal Air Force Spitfires for transport to Malta in the Mediterranean, which had been under German attack. We were warned about German and Italian subs being active in the area, and that was a little unnerving.

Well, we got through the Strait of Gibraltar without any problems, and a couple of days later, I guess, we launched the

Wildcats to function as a CAP for the Spitfires taking off from *Wasp* to reinforce Malta. Once they were off, we recovered our fighters and headed out to the Atlantic. But as fate would have it, the Germans apparently destroyed those planes on the ground right after they arrived, so we headed back to Britain for another load of Spitfires. Incredible, really. The Germans were really pounding Malta hard.

We loaded up again and went back the same way we came. We had a special guest on the *Wasp*, film star Douglas Fairbanks Jr., who was a reserve naval officer serving as the aide to the fleet admiral [Rear Admiral John L. Hall Jr.]. Our force was not a really large one, but we did have with us the HMS *Eagle*, a British carrier also carrying replacement fighters, as well as British and American destroyers. [*HMS* Eagle *was sunk by* U-73, *commanded by* Kapitänleutnant *Helmut Rosenbaum on August 11, 1942. He received the Knight's Cross for this action.*] Once we again passed Gibraltar, the lookouts got serious. We also flew missions looking for any signs of submarine activity. We again launched the Wildcats, and lost a plane and pilot who crashed on takeoff and sank. Then one of the Canadian pilots had an emergency and could not make Malta, so he had to choose landing in the sea and taking his chances or landing on the *Wasp*.

Ironically, I had discussed these types of potential problems with the RAF pilots so that they knew what to do and how to do it if they had to land aboard the ship. These were not carrier-qualified pilots, so any recovery was going to be interesting. Then it happened: the decision was made to bring him aboard, although his Spitfire was not carrier-landing equipped—he had no tailhook. Well, he came in too fast and too high and had to go around twice. The third time was the charm, although he did not stop his forward momentum until he was at the end of the flight deck. That was cutting it damned close, I can tell you. I was under the assumption that he was a very experienced pilot, given the fact that he did not go over the bow. I came to find out this was his first flight in a Spitfire.

If memory serves, he had less than two hundred hours of flight experience. I found that stunning, because you would think that flight school alone and conversion training would have given him those hours or more. He had never even done a short landing under emergency conditions either, let alone on board a carrier. I respected that guy and we pinned him with a set of gold Navy wings. Later he was picked up and they dropped him off in Gibraltar. [*The pilot was Canadian Sergeant (later Pilot Officer) Jerrold Alpine Smith (born March 26, 1921). He was later killed in action on August 10, 1942, while attacking a Ju-88 near Sicily. He would be credited with three victories and two more damaged.*]

While we were steaming back and forth to the UK, we received word about the Battle of the Coral Sea and that the *Lexington* had been sunk. [*The destroyer USS* Phelps *was ordered to sink the ship and fired a total of five torpedoes to scuttle the carrier. Some 216 crewmen were killed and 2,735 were evacuated. The carrier USS* Yorktown *was badly damaged and returned to Pearl Harbor for repairs.*] We soon received orders to return to Norfolk for refit and then continue to the Pacific as a result of our need-ing carriers in that area. We had a good escort with the battle-ship *North Carolina*, the cruisers *San Juan* and *Quincy*, and six destroyers. That must have been something to see going through the Panama Canal.

We pulled into San Diego [June 19, 1942] and heard about the Battle of Midway, where we learned the *Yorktown*, damaged in the Coral Sea, was finally sunk. But the fleet took out four Jap carriers, and along with all those aircraft and pilots, Japan was never going to recover from that ass kicking.

On the *Wasp*, we all talked about the news coming out after the Battle of Midway. The discussion also turned to the attack on Wake Island. One of our pilots had a brother in the Army in the Philippines when those fell. His family had heard nothing about their son for months. If memory serves, he is still listed as missing in action. Damned tragic, I tell you.

The standard squadron on board was between eighteen and twenty-eight planes or so, and to be combat effective, we had to have fifteen aircraft always in fighting condition. We were in-doctrinated into the Thach Weave, a new fighting maneuver invented by John [Smith] Thach just before the war. In fact, Thach scored three kills using it during the Battle of Midway, even though his flight was heavily outnumbered. The trick was to fly as slow as possible, and weave left and right, back and forth, with the other flights performing the same maneuver at staggered altitudes. Every pilot had someone covering his six at all times. This meant that regardless of which direction an attack came from, at least a couple of pilots had their guns pointed in the right direction. In most cases it was highly effective, I can tell you. I later abandoned that method because of the types of fights we got into.

Our air group consisted of a good complement of aircraft. In fact, I found the old list, so let's see: the air group, including all three carriers, had twenty-nine Wildcats, thirty Dauntlesses, and ten Avengers. That was a pretty strong air capability. We were to augment the land-based pilots who would operate on Guadalcanal and were to be joined by another task force in the future—or so we were told.

On collecting all of our new aircraft, including the fighters, torpedo and dive-bombers, our task force received orders to the Solomon Islands, where we were going to land an invasion force at Guadalcanal. *Wasp* was tasked with supporting the Marines and Army along with the rest of the task force [for Operation Watchtower]. Our task force included the [carriers] *Enterprise* and *Saratoga*, the [battleship] *North Carolina*, [six] cruisers, [sixteen] destroyers, and [five] transport ships carrying the Marines [2nd Marine Regiment]. During all of this time, until we reached the battle zone, we flew the hell out of all the aircraft, spending time in the Tonga Islands [July 18], doing cat launches and recoveries day and night to make sure we were all locked onto the program. You could never practice enough: flying off and back onto a carrier is a perishable skill.

When the battle group headed into the area on August 6, we had a strong presence with cruisers and destroyers. We closed in on the island group, and the next morning, we launched fighters and dive-bombers for the first strikes of that campaign. [*The targets in question were Tulagi, Gavutu, Tanambogo, Halavo, Port Purvis, Haleta, Bungana, and a Japanese radio station.*]

The mission was successful: the fighters nailed some float-planes and had a successful ground-attack mission. The dive-bombers took care of the antiaircraft positions. The TBFs also had a good mission supporting the Marines during the landing. We did not lose a single aircraft on those strikes, which was incredible, really. Taking the Japanese airfield was the primary objective, so we could establish a land base of operations from which to continue hitting the Japs throughout the Solomons. [*The twelve TBF Avengers, led by Lieutenant H. A. Romberg, were very effectively supporting the nineteen thousand Marines of the 1st Marine Division, who were hitting the beaches under the command of Major General Alexander A. Vandegrift. The Marines took the airfield on August 8 and named it Henderson Field.*]

The big problem for our force were the sea battles that followed. Admiral [Frank Jack] Fletcher pulled his fleet out and did not give the naval gun support that the Marines expected, and then those Marines hit some resistance. Most of this was unknown to us at the time, of course. As a result, Admiral

[Richmond K.] Turner ordered two other fleets to replace the force that left, but the Jap Navy [under Vice Admiral Gunichi Mikawa] was already there. That was what began the long-running battles at sea and allowed the Japs to land their troops in force. We called it the "Tokyo Express," and they had a strong naval presence for sure. [*Mikawa was the commander of a heavy cruiser and destroyer force that dealt a severe blow to the U.S. Navy and the Royal Australian Navy at the Battle of Savo Island on the night of August 8 to 9, 1942.*]

Our group then moved south and had the alert that a large Jap air group was headed for the transport ships resupplying Guadalcanal. The first to make contact were the SBDs when they ran into Bettys and Zeros trying to sink the transports. We had reports that the Jap Navy and their troopships were in the north, so I assumed that we would strike them soon. But that was not the case, and we spent the next few weeks patrolling. The big battle that happened on August 26 did not involve us, but the *Enterprise* was damaged bad enough to return to Pearl Harbor for repairs.

A few days later [August 31], the *Saratoga* was torpedoed and also had to return to Pearl. That left *Wasp* and *Hornet* as the two carriers in that area, which left us pretty weak. It is my understanding that most of their aircraft [from *Enterprise* and *Saratoga*] landed at Guadalcanal and started the ground-based air defense. Later there would be more air combat units stationed there. Our next job was working as escorts with the other ships and some destroyers for the transports bringing more Marines to Guadalcanal. We expected some enemy air contact soon, so we were on high alert.

My next duty assignment arrived in the form of a couple of Jap torpedoes that hit *Wasp*, and the whole ship shook. I hit the deck. It is hard to describe the feeling and sound of the explosions, and the damage was incredible. Men were killed and wounded, others blown into the sea as the life rafts were deployed and the fire was spreading. I ran to make sure that my men were off the ship before I decided it was my turn. I threw a raft off and then I jumped, and when I hit the water, it smacked hard. I went pretty deep, and when I came up, I could see the explosions. I was not wearing a flotation vest, but I never wore one on board. Some of the flight deck crew did have them as required, especially when at general quarters.

The fire on the ocean surface from the gasoline covered a large area and was spreading out to port, so I swam over to the other side and saw some of the men. There was no way we were saving that ship. Many of the men were trying to climb into the rafts. I looked around and saw a destroyer, which I assumed was coming in to rescue the crew. I had been in the water for a long time, and I had started to swim for it when I found Captain [Forest Percival] Sherman. I was really worried about the sharks. That was on my mind, as I am sure was true with all the men in the water.

After more than three hours, I was picked up by a boat sent out to rescue us [launched from the *Duncan*]. We were starting to lose daylight. The admiral [Leigh Noyes] was there and I told them where Captain Sherman was, and they picked him up along with others. *Wasp* was just a burning hulk, so she was finally sunk. That was on September 15, 1942. I remember it well. [*Japanese submarine* I-19, *commanded by Commander Takakazu Kinashi, fired six Long Lance torpedoes and three struck the* Wasp *below the waterline in the fuel and magazine holds. A third torpedo hit the destroyer USS* O'Brien, *and another hit the battleship USS* North Carolina. *Both were damaged, but neither sank.*]

Well, I can tell you that losing a ship is very demoralizing. I personally felt bad for the captain, but there is really nothing he could have done. I can't remember the exact number of casualties. It was bad, but in hindsight, it could have been a lot worse. [*Of the 2,046 crew, 197 were killed, 87 were later hospitalized, and roughly 400 were lightly injured but returned to duty.*] Some of the wounded died after being rescued, and I was tasked with handling the burials at sea. That was when I think all of this finally hit home. We were transferred to the *Helena*, where the badly wounded would be dropped off at the hospital on Espiritu Santo.

After the wounded were transferred to the hospital, I remained on board the cruiser *Helena*, which went to New Caledonia along with the *Salt Lake City* and a couple of destroyers. The one thing I had to do was get new uniforms and gear, since all of my world was at the bottom of the Pacific. I filled out the paperwork to be reimbursed. Well, all of that would have to wait while we were all loaded up on a ship and sent to San Diego to be compensated, collect our back pay, and get fitted for new uniforms. That was still going to be another wait. I was pretty pissed off, to be honest.

Then I had my orders to return to Norfolk, which was great, as all of us had earned thirty days' leave. I had been promoted to lieutenant commander in the meantime, which meant an increase in pay, of course. Plus, I could see my wife and get some rest. Well, at least I thought so. I had to go to NAS [Naval Air Station] Jacksonville as they had just consolidated the air training command. I was told they were also opening up NAS Melbourne to train more carrier pilots, and I would be sent there. Due to the war, the pace of flight training was increasing very quickly, which was to be expected. We had suffered severe losses in planes and pilots, and the war was getting hotter. We learned the *Hornet* had been sunk and that was another bitter blow for us. That hammered home the need for more pilots and trained LSOs. [*The* Hornet *was sunk on October 27, 1942, also by* I-19 *submarine.*]

This type of work was not really what I wanted to do, but the promotion to lieutenant commander that October kind of softened the blow. Postings as an instructor sometimes turned into permanent orders—purgatory really—and I dreaded that possibility. Due to my years as LSO on the *Wasp*, I was to train up new LSOs for sea duty after I got situated at Melbourne that November. The great part of that was, I was finally able to qualify in the Wildcat after all these years. I spent as much time as I could in the fighter and felt quite comfortable flying it. The six fifties were something else when doing gunnery. The whole damned plane shook, but I could see how it was effective against enemy aircraft. Now, most guys would consider this prime duty, and that was especially true if you were married. The war was not waiting, and lucky for me, I had the flight hours and rank to make the list of replacement flight leaders.

Being stateside, not in combat, would have made any wife happier than hell. I had a lot of hours, but not as many as I would have liked, due to my assignments. But flying the Wildcat was a natural thing for me. It really was a great airplane to fly. I also tried to keep up with any- and everything related to Japanese fighters, the Zero being the primary opponent. But I would also come into contact with Oscars [Nakajima Ki-43 *Hayabusa*], and later Tonys [Kawasaki Ki-61 *Hien* (Swallow)], good fighters with great characteristics. I wanted to know their strengths and weaknesses, and I was gathering a lot of valuable knowledge that would help me later, and even save my life.

You have to understand that despite the fact that it first surfaced in 1937, the Wildcat was the most advanced fighter we had in the Navy and Marine Corps until the Corsair and Hellcat came online. The first version had about a thousand horsepower engine and a top speed of just under three hundred miles an hour. It really was powerful for its day with the Pratt and Whitney air-cooled radial engine. To start those things, we used a shotgun-shell type of ignition, which the pilot fired. It made a loud-as-hell bang, too. By 1942 we had the F4F-3 in mass production, but that was a fixed-wing bird. Now we also had the Brewster Buffalo, which was a contender and in mass production. Some of the Europeans used that plane to great effect. But the Wildcat was the U.S. mainstay until 1943.

The Navy had faith in the F4F-2 after the first ones flew in 1937 and then were upgraded. They saw that it had great potential, so the Navy had Grumman make major changes to the design. The new version flew in March 1939, becoming the F4F-3. This version had a more powerful engine [Twin Wasp XR-1830-76 with a two-stage supercharger], increased wingspan and surface area, and redesigned tail surfaces, and they modified the machine-gun installation. The result was a better aircraft with much better performance and firepower. The tailplane was moved higher up the tail fin, and the profile of the vertical tail was redesigned. It had very good handling characteristics, a good roll, climb and dive rate, and better maneuverability than the previous version with a maximum speed of 335 miles an hour. After the comparative test flights the U.S. Navy ordered that model into production [August 8, 1939].

But as you may expect, design changes were always being made to all aircraft. The F4F-4 prototype was the first to have folding wings for actual carrier duty, which made perfect sense. It was the Navy, after all. That way you could stack and pack more aircraft on a carrier deck and below deck in the hangars. Of course, the Navy got those for sea duty, and by that time, they had Wright Cyclone engines, which gave more horsepower. I think that the first F4F-3 for the U.S. Navy was flown in August 1940. [*Navy Squadrons VF-7 and VF-41 received the F4F-3 at the beginning of December 1940. The U.S. Navy ordered some 95 F4F-3A aircraft with the R-1830-90 engine with single-stage supercharger, and deliveries began in 1941.*]

I remember wanting to get a slot in a Wildcat squadron, but the fates always seemed to intervene. Then the F4F-4 was introduced. It had six-fifty-caliber armament, armor pilot protection, self-sealing tanks, and the folding wing for carrier duty. This was a mount for most of the guys who were becoming Navy and Marine aces, like Foss, [Major General Marion] Carl, and those guys. Well, the Navy jumped like hell all over the improved design. Production of the F4F-4 began in November 1941 and most units had the F4F-4 by the time the Japs hit Pearl Harbor. They also upgraded the radio, and we had really good communications on those aircraft, when the radios worked. But people, especially historians, often asked how the Wildcat dealt with the Zero, which was far lighter and more maneuverable. That was where tactics came into it, like the Thach Weave.

Another thing we learned from intelligence and after-action reports was the vulnerabilities of the Zero, which by that time were well established. All the Jap fighters suffered from the same problems: they did not have self-sealing gas tanks or any armor protection for the pilot. Their guns were not up to the task like our six-fifties were, to be sure. Their lighter caliber machine guns and twenty-millimeter cannon could only do great damage to us at close range. Our fifties had greater range and better concentrated firepower. Being in a heavily armored fighter with self-sealing tanks, I felt comfortable if I went up against them. Another thing about the F4F was that the dive speed had no real redline, although a few pilots would experience compressibility in a high-speed dive.

Once you learned where that threshold was, you could avoid it by chopping power, alternating the rudder application, or lowering flaps and pulling back on the stick, or by a combination of those things. Just knowing the limitations of the fighter was life insurance, and even on its best day, no Zero could outdive a Wildcat (and especially not a Hellcat, later on) if you had full power. Hell, no Zero could outdive any American fighter in the Pacific. But they could outclimb the Wildcat and outturn it, for sure. I learned all I could about the Wildcat because we knew that the Hellcat was coming out.

By the time I was assigned to sea duty again, the Hellcat was the best naval fighter coming online, along with the Corsair, of course, which was out in 1942 to Navy and Marine fighter units. The Australians and New Zealanders also got the Corsair and they loved it, often using it as a dive-bomber and ground-attack aircraft, for which it was well suited. It could carry six five-inch rockets under the wings or two one-thousand-pound bombs, making it pretty versatile. This was where I worked the squadron up on getting proficient in dive-bombing.

Well, as you can imagine, I was pulling every string and

making every telephone call I could to try and get a combat assignment. Most of my pleas fell on deaf ears except for Commander [Ernest W.] Litch in Jacksonville. Although we did not know each other, we had both served on the *Ranger* and he was understanding. [*Litch had been the* Ranger's *navigation officer when he and McCampbell served aboard the ship.*] We also knew that a new *Hornet* designated CV-12 was being commissioned to replace the old one. They were also creating a new air group to serve aboard her, and I wanted that job. Litch made some calls, and I got my orders not long afterward. I felt like dancing.

In August of 1943, I went to NAS Atlantic City [New Jersey], where we were to train up all the pilots in a carrier group. This included the fighters, dive-bombers, and torpedo bombers who would serve together once we were assigned to a ship, which I was certain would be the new *Hornet*. The new VF-15 joined the VF-14 that was already there, using the same airfield. All of us were in Hellcats. For a number of reasons, that aircraft was really a world of difference from the Wildcat. The Japs were going to find out about that soon enough.

I was very pleased when I was assigned as squadron commander of VF-15, flying Hellcats. That was a dream job if there ever was one. One of the crazy kick-in-the-ass stories is that we had a large collection of talent—I mean, really experienced guys—as the cadre. And as luck would have it my niece [Patricia Ann O'Rourke] had a husband, an actor named Dwayne Morris, who decided to join up. He already had a private pilot's license, so he joined the Navy Reserve and got his training at Pensacola, the old stomping ground. He had been stuck in Kansas and wanted to fly fighters, so I did what I could and had him assigned to the training cadre with me. He was already a qualified flight instructor anyway.

I can tell you that I worked those guys every hour of daylight. I was heavy on navigation because the ocean has no landmarks, so they learned everything there was to learn about instrument flying. We did all the carrier takeoff and landing exercises, gunnery, dogfighting, tight- and combat-formation flying, simulated ground attacks—everything you would expect a fighter pilot to have to do in combat. Combat was what we wanted, and I wanted those guys prepared so they could stay alive.

That concept had an interesting twist, because in anticipation of serving aboard the new *Hornet*, I met with the new CO of the ship, Captain Miles [Rutherford] Browning. We discussed VF-15 and the training, all that shit, and he told me not to train my fighter pilots to dive-bomb. Well, let's just say that that piece of advice was rapidly forgotten. I wanted my pilots trained in *every* aspect of air warfare. I think he was probably more concerned with the possibility of losing good fighter pilots because they were performing a role better suited to the Dauntless dive-bombers that we would be flying cover for.

In flight training, and especially in advanced flight school, where the requirements are more demanding and dangerous, you expect to have some losses. I did not want to have any fatalities or lose aircraft, but I did push the men hard. I knew they would need it. We did lose two pilots in crashes and the cause was never confirmed in either case. [*The two pilots were Ensign J. A. Wakefield and Ensign D. F. Hoffman.*] By November, when we had orders to relocate to Pungo [near Virginia Beach], which was part of NAS Norfolk, I thought they were a good unit. That was the same month the new *Hornet* was commissioned. We were just waiting for orders to load up and ship out.

In the meantime, VB-15 was also formed up as part of the air group. They had been using the Dauntless and were now using Helldivers. That fact meant transition training that cost them a lot of time. None of the pilots were really up to speed on flying that beast, and none of them liked that aircraft [the Helldiver] for a lot of good reasons. The Avenger pilots were also trained and formed up. I had to make a tough call, so I whittled the number of pilots down to the forty that I could take. Once all was well and good, we began qualifications on the escort carrier USS *Long Island*.

We finally completed all that and joined *Hornet* in January for the shakedown cruise, which was all of three weeks. It was not very long, but we maximized the time and did a lot of flying. We had a lot of problems with the Helldiver squadron. There were crashes, some fatalities, guys banging up on the flight deck, all because the Helldiver needed a lot more deck to land on. Once that was rectified, the accidents stopped. The ship's captain [Browning] was pretty pissed off that shit was happening, and I understood his position. It did not look too damned good to keep writing off bombers and pilots when we were not even in combat.

Browning was pretty heavy-handed and micromanaged everything, which did not sit well with us three squadron commanders or the group commander. In fact, when we returned to port, Browning relieved both the commander of Air Group 15 [Commander William M. Drane] and the squadron commander [Lieutenant Commander Irwin L. Dew] of their duties. Guess who was appointed the new air group commander. You got it. That was my new promotion, and my XO, Charlie Brewer, became squadron leader for VF-15. Despite all of that, I actually got along rather well with Browning personally. That was probably because none of my guys had killed themselves or scattered wreckage across his flight deck.

Before we departed the ship, Captain Browning thought enough of my judgment to ask me for recommendations as a replacement squadron commander for the bombers. After some juggling [Lieutenant Commander] James [Haile] Mini came aboard and took charge. The problem was that he had never flown a Helldiver, so he had a very quick learning curve. He did pretty well, considering that imposing problem. Later we had [Lieutenant Commander] Val [Valdemar G.] Lambert, who was a former flight instructor himself. We took some shore leave while *Hornet* was having work done but were back on board and headed to the Pacific on Valentine's Day 1944.

We took the usual route south, heading into the Caribbean,

but we lost a Helldiver and others were damaged in rough seas as we passed Cape Hatteras. We still did a lot of practice missions, and we lost another one over Panama. Such was the nature of the job, I guess, but it is always tragic when you lose someone, especially in a noncombat-related event. We hit San Diego and were next in Hawaii the first week of March. Then the shit got strange. Apparently, Browning filed his reports about VB-15, which I could only assume were less than glowing, and the Navy brass decided that our group was not combat ready. One of the ax-grinding issues was that they wanted the Hellcat pilots dive-bombing proficient, but this was not allowed under Browning, as I mentioned. As a result, we left the *Hornet* and were sent ashore for further training.

We spent almost two months there. I had little command and control over our pilots and crews, as the base commander took a great interest in our conduct. Many of the bombers' problems were small technical issues that we got worked out. It just came down to the squadron getting more familiar with the Helldiver. It was a bitch to fly and was not what I would call today a user-friendly unit. It looked like we would never even get near combat.

One thing we worked on was dropping bombs from the Hellcats. The current doctrine was for fast fighters to slip in and hit airfields by dropping bombs and strafing aircraft and structures, whatever was available as a target. During training we lost two Hellcats and both pilots. After this, I modified our combat tactics, only using the Thach Weave in rare circumstances when a pilot was in serious trouble. As it worked out later, that was a good move. Once we were formed up and considered trained, we had orders to return to Pearl Harbor. In April we loaded up and boarded the [USS] *Essex*, joining her torpedo and dive-bomber squadrons. We were heading hard into the war.

The *Essex* was the first ship in the fleet carrier class, and one of the biggest we built during the war. [*Weighing twenty-seven thousand tons, the Essex was 820 feet long and carried twenty-six hundred men.*] On board were VF-15 flying the Hellcats, VB-15 flying the Helldivers, and VT-15 flying the Avengers as the torpedo bomber unit. A formidable task force to be sure. We were highly motivated; you cannot overestimate the enthusiasm we had, and we were eager to get into combat. *Essex* had already been battle tested in the fighting in the Marshall Islands, the Marianas, Makin, Kwajalein, Rabaul, Tinian, Wake, Saipan, Guam, all the major operations throughout 1943 and the first quarter of 1944. My CAG-15 [commander-carrier air group] was to replace CAG-9, who had been exhausted by the time their tour was over.

Life aboard the *Essex* was much better than aboard the *Hornet* because I had command authority over my group, and the squadron leaders were not being monitored all the damned time. The ship's captain, Ralph [Andrew] Ofstie, was an old-time pilot who understood the way a good flying unit operated. He had a hands-off policy where we were concerned. In fact, we rarely saw him. He left us alone to do our jobs and morale rose as a result. While life and morale were better than we expected, we did not have air-conditioning, and the heat and humidity were pretty stifling. Hardly anyone wore a flight suit; it was just too damned hot.

We landed all the aircraft without incident, which made me breathe a little easier. [*CAG-15 had 122 pilots, thirty-seven Hellcats, thirty-six Helldivers, twenty Avengers, and six F6F-3N night fighters attached from VF-77.*] We also had a good relationship with the XO [Commander David L. McDonald], who openly welcomed us aboard. All loaded up, we set sail for the Marshall Islands with a task force including the new *Wasp, San Jacinto*, with cruisers *Reno* and *San Diego* and our destroyer escorts. [*The destroyers were USS* Henley, Dyson, Charles Ausburne, Converse, Wadleigh, *and* Spence.]

As was standard operational procedure, we were constantly flying, practicing night and day and becoming more proficient. We were soon briefed on the mission at hand: the fleet was supporting the invasion of the Mariana Islands, with the objective of capturing the islands and airfields. This would place the Army Air Force bases much closer to Japan, which would soon put the new B-29 Superfortress heavy bombers in striking range of the Japanese home islands. We were nowhere near the time for the Marianas operation, so the powers that be thought we needed some combat. I personally thought that was a great idea, and the rest of the men agreed. The fleet sailed to Marcus Island, where the Japs were still hanging on.

I got into a standard routine, such as always attending the S-2 briefings for my fighters and sitting in on the overall info, but I let bomber squadron commanders handle their own affairs. I think it reduces a leader's effectiveness with his men if he is always being overlorded by his superior, so I drank my coffee and caught up on private business. We held classes on aircraft recognition, ship recognition, going over routes, that kind of thing.

We flew our combat missions [178 sorties] over Marcus Island and all those small islands in May [19 and 20, 1944]. Our group had very few contacts and only a couple of kill claims. The bombers did a great job, and our fighters strafed a lot of shit on the ground and worked the AA guns over, giving the bombers some security. I flew these missions, and as some Hellcats hit the guns, the rest flew CAP to make sure that no unwanted enemy fighters came to join the show. We did not lose many planes, only two fighters and two bombers. Some came back damaged [eleven in total], but there were no other write-offs. We did lose a Hellcat and the pilot was my wingman, [Ensign] Wesley [Thomson] Burnham. He had been hit by ground fire and burned in. One Helldiver flown by [Ensign] Jared [H.] Dixon also went down along with his gunner [ARN2c Sam Hogue]. I listed them as missing, but nothing more at that time.

After I lost Burnham, [Lieutenant (JG)] Roy Rushing became my new wingman for the rest of my time with the ship. Our next area after refueling was Wake Island. When we reached the station, we launched five of the strikes [146 sorties], losing a Hellcat and pilot. Another Helldiver ditched, but the crew were recovered. We had destroyer rescue on station and a submarine also, and the fighters flew CAP to cover those recoveries. The next adventure was the attack in the Marianas. By this time the Japs were getting screwed at every turn. Our subs had been sinking their transport ships, which were carrying troops to reinforce their island empire after losing the Marshall Islands. As Task Force 58 we were going to finish the job. This was called Operation Forager and it was a massive fleet.

One of my responsibilities was to read the AARs to check the damage reported by the bombers and review for confirmation any claims for aircraft shot down. I was pretty strict, and a claimed kill was just that unless there was another eyewitness to the event. That was the way it had always been. Damaged claims were just that. I considered a kill probable until verified. A few of the fighters were fitted with gun cameras, but these were somewhat problematic, so I had them all removed. There were several good reasons for this action, the most prevalent being that the fighter pilots would get target fixation and want to follow a kill to get it on camera. This meant dropping below the hard deck, which made them vulnerable. In addition, it was not unusual for more than one fighter to hit the same enemy, and the cameras would also fail on occasion.

I also stressed that I wanted each pilot to fly his own personal aircraft, which was to be maintained by his own crew chief. That way, we had total accountability and pilots developed a special bond with their chief mechanics. I always told my guys to treat their plane captains and mechanics with special respect. They have your life in their hands, and they look to you to make them look good by getting back with a well-performing machine. I have spoken to pilots from different countries, and all told me the same thing. A pilot without a good ground crew, especially a good chief mechanic, was just another guy looking for something to do. My crew chief actually made me a cigarette holder in my cockpit and kept a fresh pack of Lucky Strikes in there for me.

I led the first air attacks on Saipan [June 11]. We dropped bombs and then strafed, preparing for the bombers. I took the role of air boss readily, coordinating the attacks from my perch. We had aircraft from several carriers, and it was some show, especially when Brewer destroyed a whole group of seaplanes with a bomb. We hit the island hard, and I got my first air kill when I saw a Zero attacking a few Hellcats. I dropped my auxiliary tank, pulled into him, and fired. He went in and sank. Many of the fighter pilots were getting kills. I could hear them over the radio. The thing I learned was that in the hands of a good pilot, the Zero was basically dead meat when confronted by a Hellcat. They learned that the hard way.

The next day we did more sweeps, hitting targets, the airfield, and some cargo ships. We also managed to engage a large Jap convoy, and as the fighters flew cover, the bombers hit them hard. A couple were sunk and almost all were badly damaged. We landed and launched again. The bombers on this second sortie were armed with rockets instead of bombs. Once again, the Japs lost a few ships. Once the bombers were done, we strafed the remaining ships. But we were not yet done. After the bombers did their runs, we hit them again and blew up a Jap destroyer—incredible really, and this lasted for days. I had my second kill during that period.

We kept getting vectored into Jap bombers, Bettys mostly, and a few fighters here and there. The Japs were seriously trying to hit the fleet, which was what I would do. Their problem was that we were always able to get the alert from the radar contacts, get a CAP overhead, and then jump on them. We swept them from the sky every time. By the time that was over, the Japs had lost a lot of ships and planes, not to mention irreplaceable pilots.

Our next major effort was supporting the landings on Iwo Jima, which was strategically critical where the bombing campaign was concerned. During these sweeps [starting on June 15, 1944], we collectively shot down almost thirty fighters. Then we strafed the airfield and just beat the shit out of the area, destroying planes on the ground and hitting buildings and such. The AA fire was predictably heavy. Some of our fighters were hit and a couple of men like Lieutenant George [Ralph] Crittenden were wounded. He was shot in the left leg but landed safely aboard the *Essex*.

By the time the dive-bombers entered the fray after we had softened up the airfield, the gunners who were still active were fully alerted and waiting for them. I really had a bad feeling about the bombers, given the never-ending volumes of fire coming up at us. They got hit badly, and we lost some planes and crews. Some of them were observed crashing into the sea and climbing into life rafts, but when rescuers arrived in the area, none of these men were ever located. That hit pretty hard. The next day was more of the same. The weather was shit, but we thought that would be to our advantage, and it was. The Japs never even came up, and with all the carriers sending up their fighters and bombers, there was no opposition. It was a major effort, and I think we destroyed another sixty or so Jap planes on the ground.

When it was all over, the tally was fifty-four enemy aircraft in the air. I think about thirty were destroyed by the bombers on the airfield. After we were done, the big naval guns began bombarding, throwing heavy shells. The Marines were stretched very thin with Iwo and Saipan going on, and of course both required air support. I think it was [Lieutenant] Bob Maxwell who became our first ace [for VF-15] during these operations. Then we went back to Saipan, as problems there were still ongoing. But things were going to get more interesting.

A week later we were engaged against a large Jap carrier-based force in the Philippine Sea. We were alerted that they were incoming toward the fleet, and we were one of the fighter groups acting as a defensive screen to protect them. We also learned it was a large Jap fleet with carriers. That meant more planes, not just land-based bitches. Our first contacts by VF-15 were good, and we collected some scalps. We could hear the Hellcat pilots calling out visuals and kills without stopping. A few Japs got through, but did not manage to do anything to the ships, except for the *South Dakota,* which had some casualties. [*Vice Admiral Jisaburō Ozawa dispatched sixty-nine fighters and bombers and lost forty-nine in the first day of battle. Ozawa's flagship, the carrier* Taihō, *was sunk by the submarine USS* Albacore. *He also lost the carrier* Shōkaku, *which was sunk by another submarine, the USS* Cavalla.]

We took off. I had twelve Hellcats in the air when we found some Judys [Yokosuka D4Y, "Comet"] far below us, about a mile down. I led the attack as we dropped from about twenty thousand feet. I locked onto one of the last bombers, blew his ass apart, then pulled around and fired at the lead bomber and got him also. While this was going on, my wingman shot one down after he had taken some damage, and we both headed back to the *Essex.* I could hear so many calls for kills, it was amazing, and quite a few damaged fighters were coming back to the ship. This latest engagement was epic by any standard. [*Of the 128 Japanese aircraft sent out during this second mission, 97 were shot down.*]

The Japs were not quite done, I guess, because we had another mission. Again, the fighters engaged, and again, we had great results. Then intel came in that the remaining Jap aircraft were flying to the islands. We dozen fighters joined to cover the bombers and hit any fighters while the bombers hit the airfield at Guam. As we closed in, I shot down a Zeke, but took some damage, as did my wingman at the time [Ensign Royce L. Nall], who was chewed up pretty badly by two Zeros. I got one and hit another, but that was only a damaged Jap. Then my wingman disappeared from view, but I had Japs all over the place.

I looked over and saw two seaplanes with some Corsair cover on a rescue for our pilots. I decided to get involved while they flew CAP, but then it was time to head back since everyone broke off. A previous fighter flight that had taken off before we returned also had success and shot down a few Zeros. That last big fight of the Turkey Shoot [June 19] had the unit credited with almost seventy kills, but it was an expensive success. We lost thirteen Hellcat pilots from the combined fleet, another dozen or so aircrew and [thirty] sailors. Sadly, we also lost both Brewer and his wingman [Ensign Thomas Tarr].

We were headed back near Saipan, where we refueled from the tankers, then prepared to hit Guam. Once done, we resumed air operations. I took the seventeen Hellcats on the first strike early in the morning on June 20. Far down below were four bandits, but I decided to keep on our heading. We hit the field and were headed back when we saw these guys again, and the flight engaged. One was shot down, but the rest got lucky. At least we fired up a Jap transport ship. We had no losses and landed without any problems. Then we got ready for the next mission and launched twenty fighters with a bombload. Once they had done their bomb and strafing run, they ran into Zeros and we lost a Hellcat and pilot [Ensign J. W. Power].

I think it was the next day that the *Wasp* pilots and those from other carriers located the enemy fleet with their carriers and launched a devastating attack on the Japs. They lost some ships and aircraft, but they were far from beaten, and our fleet did not fare much better when it came to the air groups. On return, the guys had to land at night, damaged and low on fuel. It was hell and most of the losses were from landing after the battle. I scratched my head on that one. [*The battle cost the fleet four Avengers, six Hellcats, and ten Helldivers, but another seventeen Hellcats, twenty-eight Avengers, and thirty-five Helldivers were lost after the battle in crashes on decks or ditching due to lack of fuel while awaiting a landing.*]

Well, my air group was still busy with Guam and Saipan at that time. The Helldivers took a beating and we lost another crew. The bombers did attack gun positions and crater the runway. We were on a sweep to hit the Guam airfield again, when we saw some Zeros on the runway and others with camo nets off to the side. It looked like this flight was rolling, since they were taking off, so I called in to hold off on the ground attack. Looking back, I then saw that the flight of four was at our altitude, about fifteen thousand feet, and they dropped very low and went into a defensive circle.

I left four of my twelve fighters as high cover and we went in to hit them. As soon as I made that call, we had [six] Zeros come in out of the sun and attack, so my top four rolled over to engage them as we hit the lower element. I smoked one and he blew up, but when I banked back into the battle, we had eight Zeros now. Then I locked onto another one and he just smoked and plunged down. But another one was running away below, so I went in after him. I fired and he rolled away smoking, but then I had one on my six. I called for help, but he disappeared. I flew back over the airfield [Orote], where a friendly parachute had been seen and called out, but there were no bandits in the sky. It was rather chaotic over the radio, and we headed back to the ship. After landing, I learned we had chalked up eleven Zekes, but two fighters failed to return [Lieutenant (JG) J. L. Bruce and Lieutenant R. L. Stearns].

Another mission took us back to the airfield again. The bombers hit it and some buildings, and the fighters strafed, but there was no air resistance. The third mission was a little more involved. When the Helldivers went back to hit the airfield this time, the Japs had some air cover. That was a good day for me, as I had ten confirmed air victories by that time [June 23, 1944]. But we hit that bastard again the next day, really pounding Guam.

We launched at sunrise and once we were over the target area, we saw a transport ship and a troop carrier. We fighters hit the troop carrier and the dive-bombers hit the transport ship, and the troop boat sank. Meanwhile other groups joined in the fray, hitting both airfields [Orote and Agana]. This happened a couple of times that day. Intelligence confirmed that the Japs were in fact reinforcing Guam in a big way.

The next few weeks were rather mundane. The Army and Marines had finally taken Saipan, so we were gearing up for the expansion into the Marianas. We would be dividing our time between still hitting Guam and hitting Tinian, where major landings were going to take place. The bombers had the most action over the next few days since there was no real Jap air presence, but the flak was doing some damage for sure. By mid-August Tinian, Guam, and Saipan were all American-held territory.

After a full week of just letting the bombers pound these islands, we headed for the Philippines. On September 9, we launched the first strikes against Mindanao. Fighters and bombers wrecked the airfields and hit their supply dumps and a Jap transport convoy. All of the air groups worked it over, sinking a few ships and damaging a hell of a lot of others. I think we flew three missions that day, a good day to be sure. But not having good maps with airfields or other critical targets plotted was a major problem, so I sent the squadrons out to snoop around and fire up whatever they found. They were to make sure they plotted the coordinates of whatever they found so we would know where these places were, because we had no damned idea. We were flying every day, just hitting anything we could find.

September 12 was a great day because we hit several islands [Negros, Panay, Cebu, Leyte, Samar, Bohol, Masbate, and Mactan]. We targeted their airfields and shot up many Japs caught on the ground and destroyed many others as they were taking off or lining up to take off. Several fighters that did get off the ground were shot down. I led the strike force with fifteen Hellcats and a few Avengers and Hellcats, and the group sank a couple of cargo ships and barges and destroyed oil and fuel facilities and a few aircraft on the ground. After we landed, we examined the strike photos and then went back.

My second launch was to hit shit we had missed, which was not much in my opinion, because we could still see the fire and smoke from the first strike. We did more damage with bombs and rockets, and the dive-bombers did good work on a couple of cargo ships they went after. I called it in and got back to the *Essex* to get ready for a third mission that just inflicted more damage. I felt good about the day's events, as I had four more kills. I think the group had twenty-seven all totaled, but we did lose some more aircraft, pilots, and crews.

The next day we were escorting the bombers, so I led a flight of Hellcats from both *Essex* and *Lexington* on a jaunt to Negros Island. We hit some Jap planes on the ground and one of my guys splashed a couple of Bettys. We were on station as cover when we saw inbound bandits, and I flamed an Oscar. The Japs had the altitude advantage staggered a few thousand feet above us. We climbed into the oncoming Japs, and I managed to nail a Kate [Nakajima B5 torpedo (bomber)], and another went burning in from another pilot. Then I saw a Nate [Nakajima Ki-27] that disappeared into the clouds, but I also saw another group above me. I rocked my wings as they approached, but all of them came in, so I dove and dragged their asses lower where my Hellcats were waiting for them. Then it was game on. Everyone was involved in that fight. There were more Nates and I hit one, but he went into the clouds also. We had been flying awhile and were low on gas, so I called us back to the *Essex*.

In all, we had about sixty to seventy planes in the air [thirty-three from *Essex*] on average during the four strikes we launched. We had shot down quite a few. I do not remember exactly how many, but I do know that the task force in total had nailed about 170 planes in the air and over 300 on the ground, and the bomber pilots sank over 50 ships in two days. We did all of this with the loss of only eight of our aircraft. Others were damaged and we had men wounded, but aside from that, it was a great week for us.

The next major strike was on September 21, when we took all of our groups in two waves to give the Japs hell at Manila and the surrounding area. Once again, we were going for airfields and other targets. We had reports of big ships in the area, so our bombers had torpedoes. After that mission we returned, refueled, and rearmed, and I took off again at full strength. We were flying the F6F-5 and carrying rockets and bombs, so when we located a Jap convoy, we rolled in to hit first, so we would be free to fly CAP and cover the bombers. I fired rockets into a cargo ship, and it just stopped moving. The Helldivers did a better job with their torpedoes. The fourth strike that went out was a good one. The bombers sank a few ships, finishing off some damaged by the previous missions. This battle was really just getting started.

The next morning [September 22], we took off full strength

again and those of us with the new Hellcats had rockets and flew above the bombers. *Lexington*'s group joined up with us. I was at twelve thousand watching the effects of the bombing mission, when we saw a twin-engine Jap bomber above us at maybe twenty thousand feet. I wanted to get him, so we poured on the coals as we climbed to reach it. Once I got close enough, I decided that since I had not fired my five-inch rockets, I would give it a shot, so I fired a couple and damaged him. He tried to get away, but I think I had done enough damage with the rockets to let me close in on him. When I fired the guns, his right engine lit up and the wing separated, so it flipped right in. My VF-15 hit a Jap submarine at dock and seriously damaged it. The end result from all the bomber squadrons was about seventeen ships sunk, including a destroyer. We then rendezvoused to refuel the ships, so we had a couple of days to rest, and we needed it.

Once we were back on station, we prepared to launch a major strike. On September 24, just about every plane from every carrier was in the air. My target was Cebu Harbor. We then came across two seaplanes that the pilots from my flight shot down. We launched strikes throughout the day with good results, managing to hit everything still floating from the previous missions. That was a short campaign. We had done a great job and I was very proud of my men. I had nineteen kills by the end of September, and the unit was racking up a great total.

October was going to be busy. We were tasked with hitting Okinawa—the airfields and anything floating. On the tenth, my wingman [Rushing] and I had rockets and we hit four cargo ships, good hits. The main force of fighters and bombers hit the airfields. That first strike caught them off guard. Their second mission was not so smooth since the Japs were alerted and sent their fighters up. I was over the channel directing the bombers to their targets. They dropped torpedoes, hitting some barges, while the other group paid the airfield [Yontan Air Base] another visit. At the end of the day, I think the entire task force had lost twenty-one planes, five pilots, and four airmen, not including the wounded. But we had destroyed a lot of planes and ships and ass-crippled the Japs.

The next day, we launched into a mission against Luzon. There was no air activity, and we hit ground targets including a dozen Jap bombers. Out of sixty-one planes, we lost seven. This was the last blow in that area for a while because we were soon to be involved in the fighting over Formosa, called Taiwan today. That operation had all of our groups in the air. When the first flight arrived, the Japs had their fighters ready and flying above us, so we had to climb to reach them. At about twenty thousand feet or so, fighters were suddenly all over the sky. It was furious—everything the Japs had in their fighter inventory was up there.

The radio traffic was hard to catch due to jamming, but I could tell that Japs were falling in flames all over. Parachutes were called out, not many, but they were Japs. While the top fighters were engaged, the ground-attack element went to the airfields. I led the first strike on Kobi Airfield. We fired rockets and strafed the aircraft we saw—Bettys, maybe some Vals, and the like—then climbed to cover the bombers for their run. We returned and launched a second strike and sank four small ships by strafing and firing rockets, but I had no air contacts. The third and fourth strikes were also devastating to the Japanese. All the carrier air groups really beat the hell out of them.

We repeated the same the next day. The weather had turned bad. *Lexington's* planes did good work, but there was not much that I could do. We did a second launch with little effect, but we lost several fighters and bombers and their pilots and crews as well. A few Jap bombers broke through, trying to attack the ships, but were shot down. The only real issue was that one bomber dropped a torpedo that hit the *Canberra* and she had to be towed.

The next day [October 14], the Japs attacked the fleet in force. That shit lasted all day, with hundreds of Jap torpedo and dive-bombers coming in, wave after wave. The *Houston* was hit bad but taken under tow like the *Canberra*. Then *Houston* was hit again the next day by a torpedo. I remember having several discussions about Japanese losses. We wondered how many more planes they could still have left after all the shit we had shot down and destroyed on the ground.

We left that area for a fleet refueling and damage assessment, and then steered to the Philippines again. The morning of October 21, Rushing and I took off, followed by the group. We directed the bombers to a ship we saw, and then we saw two

Nates, and we both got one each. Not long after, I saw a twin-engine Jap and shot that down. The radio chatter was full of my fighter pilots hitting Japs in the air battle that followed. The bombing and strafing also went off well. We did not see any more real activity until the twenty-third, when the entire strike force was engaged in a battle that lasted until the next day. The task force fighters had done a great job clearing the skies, but some Jap bombers still came in, and the *Princeton* was badly damaged.

October 24, 1944, was a day to remember for sure. We were still in the Philippine Sea and had been sending out fighter sweeps. It was always good to know if the enemy was in the air beyond our radar capability. That morning we had radar contacts, a lot of bogeys incoming from due west. I had some of my fighters already up doing reconnaissance in the area around Manila. Admiral [Marc] Mitscher on the *Lexington* notified the fighters already airborne as to the alert status. Radar had about eighty incoming bandits and every fighter in the task force was airborne, as you can imagine. We had some trouble coming in. I think every fighter from every carrier was up and in the air except me, and I was a little pissed off.

I heard that they had stumbled across the entire Jap fleet, including a few battleships. I knew that the dive- and torpedo bombers would be having a field day. We learned later that my group had sunk the *Musashi* and really hurt other ships. This was incredible news. [*This was the Imperial Japanese Navy's Central*

Fleet under the command of Vice Admiral Takeo Kurita.] Our fighter screen wiped out half of the Jap aircraft coming in— they simply destroyed half of that entire force. Those Jap planes never got near the ships.

Well, then the call went out for all pilots to man their planes and we hustled to the Hellcats, but I was then handed the message to stand down. I had returned to my quarters when we received another call for action, so I just figured this was a new directive. I climbed in as they were fueling me up. I was again ordered to stand down, if memory serves, but I was already on the launch profile. They already had the ship headed into the wind, and I was hooked up for launch. I did not have a full fuel load either, but I could not wait. The fueling crew was waved off and I gave the wave and was shot down the deck and off I went.

My wingman, Roy Rushing, took off right after me. Then my five fighters that were still on board joined us. As I said, the rest were doing sweeps. Once we reached altitude, we spotted the incoming aircraft, so I called it in. I wanted to know if we had friendlies in the area. Better to know that before you get up close and personal with incoming aircraft, you know? When the response was negative, I knew we were getting into a fight. That also meant that the fleet would be in danger, and we were always the first line of defense.

What we were seeing was a combined force of bombers, torpedo bombers, and their escort fighters—an impressive force. My late arrivals were below us and I gave the order for them to hit the bombers. Rushing and I climbed and managed to get into a good position just above and behind the enemy fighters. When they entered that stupid Vic formation, it was time to go in. I gave the order and rolled into the attack, hitting a fighter at the tail end of their formation. I closed fast and had him in a perfect sight picture. Fire and flames shot out as he tumbled down. I did not see the pilot get out.

I saw Roy score a kill, but I also saw that my other planes were engaging the bombers. It almost seemed as if the fighters had no idea what was going on or what had just happened. Good coms helps a team be more effective, but I had heard that many Jap planes did not have radios to extend their range. If they were flying this mission without communications, then they were seriously screwed. This seemed to be the case, because I locked onto another Zero who seemed unaware of the events, and shot him down. Then they got smart and went into a Lufbery. Well, perhaps not completely smart. That formation was used as a defensive measure. Flying in a big circle, each pilot was protected by the guy behind him from attack.

Roy and I climbed, watching this, and then I rolled into the attack. I fired at one and he fired back. We zoomed past each other, both taking a few hits, but I was fine. Roy had the same experience but no great effect. I assumed that they might be low on fuel. The enemy bombers were nowhere to be seen and I heard that they had been scattered. The enemy fighters broke out of the circle and headed back the way they came, which was Manila, but we did not leave them alone.

We stayed engaged for a long time, maybe an hour and a half, and a lot of radio calls later, we finally got some support. We climbed high and then rolled into the attack at high speed, each selecting a target. It was shoot, bank away left and right, and climb. My second target fell away smoking and went down. Once we reached perch, we would look down and select the next victims. We did it again and I bagged a third and Roy also got one. I did it again and closed in on an Oscar, I think, but as I fired, I saw tracers fly past my wing, so I pulled up. One of my guys was firing at the same Jap, which kind of pissed me off, but I returned to that guy, and he went down. I called out my fourth kill so far. I was feeling pretty good, to be honest.

I scored two more, an Oscar or a Hamp, I think, and a Zero, calling them out, and confirmations came over the radio. Roy had five, I think, to my six. But the problem was my fuel was low, and we were following these clowns farther northwest. I caught another straggler and sent him down. Even though Roy had plenty of fuel, I would be in serious shit soon, and unable to make the carrier. It would be even worse if we were met by more Japs coming to the rescue. Then I closed on another and fired. He smoked, but as I pulled up, I did not see Roy.

I looked around and saw a fighter closing in on me from my six. I felt relieved when I learned it was my wingman. He radioed that he was out of ammo, but he said he would follow me in as I went to hit the Japs once again. I locked onto another straggler and went into him, closed in, and fired. Half my guns went dry, but I hit him enough. He just lit up like a bonfire and went down to the sea. I did not see a parachute from any of the eight that I shot down. I was ready to head back when I saw another straggler below me, so I again closed in and fired, and he smoked badly and went down. Again, the pilot did not bail out. Roy and I were both out of ammo, and I was dangerously low on fuel, so going back to the *Essex* was the only option. In fact, I was worried about even making it back. I had not really sweated during the entire battle, but now I was feeling it.

I radioed that I had to land, and I was informed by the *Essex* that the deck was full on a launch, and it would be a while. I told them that I did not have a while and began looking around. I called in to the other ships. We closed in on *Hornet* and they fired at us. Apparently, they were trigger-happy after the recent events. No sooner did I call in a cease-fire than a flight of Hellcats came in on us, ready for action. They recognized us, so that was one positive outcome.

We passed by *Essex* but the flight deck was full since they were still in the process of launching. I was dry and prepared to ditch when I called in to *Lexington*. I saw their flight deck was packed before they even responded, but *Langley* said clear. That gave me hope, as my fuel gauge read zero. I came in after a hard banking turn. The engine coughed and died, and I bounced and trapped the second wire. I was safe but sweaty as hell, I can tell you. I was also out of gas. I had minor damage to the Hellcat, but it was rearmed and refueled, so I was good to go pretty soon afterward. The best part was that we did not lose a single fighter or pilot. Those were the best missions—when everyone came home.

My pilots landed on the various ships. After being serviced, I was up again with them running a CAP, as there was still the threat of torpedo or dive-bombers coming in. We cruised around but had no contacts. I guessed the Japs had taken enough of a beating for the day. After we were done, we were able to return to the *Essex*. I was in a little trouble because the admiral [Rear Admiral Frederick C. Sherman] did not want me flying scrambles. But at least I had a defender, his aide [Captain Charles R.] Brown, who reminded him that I was there to fight Japs and had done a good job. I was congratulated on the mission and for the nine kills.

We had prevented a large force of about sixty Japs from reaching the fleet. I guess that fact eased some of the anger directed at me for violating the admiral's orders. We had engaged and owned the day. I shot down nine, Rushing had six, and others did very well also. This became known as the Marianas Turkey Shoot. I know that Alex Vraciu had also got six flying from the *Lexington* the previous June. That made big news, but now I had the lead on kills per mission.

The next morning, I led a large force of over a hundred planes from the *Essex*, *Langley*, and *Lexington*, looking for Jap ships. Rushing and I stayed high to cover and direct traffic, and ten Hellcats that went in with bombs saw a Jap carrier launching planes. My Helldivers and Avengers were excellent: they sank a carrier, damaged another, and sank a destroyer, all in that one strike, and the torpedoes hit a battleship. Then the second strike came in and picked up where the first group left off. More Jap ships were smoking when the third wave launched and caught up with the rest of the fleet attacking the ships that had not been hit yet. They hit another carrier, the *Zuikaku*, which had led the Pearl Harbor attack, and that big bitch also went down. By the time I returned to the ship with my group, the fourth strike was on their way to inflict more punishment.

After our air strikes successfully damaged, sunk, or slowed down a large part of the Jap fleet, our surface ships caught up with them. That kicked off the largest sea battle in history, and it was expensive in planes, ships, and lives. But on October 26, we were still searching for the remaining Jap ships. I sent four Hellcats out, a couple of two-man elements for a look and see. One of the teams radioed in that they had a dozen Zeros escorting Judys and Jills [B6N *Tenzan*, "Heavenly Mountain"] that were obviously coming for the fleet. The team effectively engaged, shooting the fighters down and forcing the bombers to reverse course and head back. Great job there.

Not long afterward we began experiencing kamikaze attacks. These crazy bastards hit the carriers *Intrepid*, *Belleau Wood*, and *Franklin*. The next day the destroyers *Ammen* and *Claxton* were also hit. [*The destroyer* Abner Read *was sunk by a kamikaze as well.*] I had sixty-eight planes in the air on November 5 as the force struck the airfields in Manila. I had managed to shoot down a Val when my wingman [Rushing] and I saw a pair of Zeros below headed toward us, so we rolled over into a dive and got on their tails. We each got one, but both of us had gun problems when we saw more Zeros in the distance.

Although our guns were of no use, we stayed on station until the second strike came in, and then we headed back to the *Essex*. The reports sent the bombers out again, and one of my Avenger pilots [Lieutenant R. D. Cosgrove] lost his gunner [L. E. Dean], whom he brought back dead aboard the ship. After last rites, he was buried at sea still trapped in the aircraft. The alarm sounded that more kamikazes were coming in. They were engaged, but one hit the *Lexington*, killing a lot of men. By the end of the day, all the reports confirmed that the Japs still had a lot of planes and ships in the bay.

The next day I led the group as the coordinator on another anti-shipping flight with about seventy aircraft. Although there was no air contact to speak about, the group torpedoed and bombed some ships and plastered the airfield, destroying some bombers on the ground by just basically tearing shit up like they always did. We then had a couple of days of well-earned downtime. But on November 11, I think, we went in with the largest combined air group that had ever been formed up to that time. We had lost a few fighters and bombers. As you can imagine, losing men was the toughest part, but we still had a job to do.

That morning, despite the bad weather, we were to locate and hit the transport ships to stop them from landing troops and shit. From what I heard, the Japs had dumped close to forty thousand soldiers in there. That's a lot of rice bowls, and we were to sink anything that could supply them. I was circling high above, directing traffic after we spotted four large transports. I had directed the dive- and torpedo bombers in to hit them, when suddenly this Jap [Oscar] flew by. I turned to get him, and he went in after a few minutes. As that was going on, the Hellcats dropped down to strafe and drop their bombs, followed by the bombers. One ship was sunk outright, and the rest took solid hits. But after they did their runs, more bandits came in and the fight was on. Both sides took hits, and by the time the action finally broke off, we had lost seven planes. The rest of the task force did well in sinking some destroyers and more transports.

Well, as a result of the nature of that mission—which, by the way, was the worst single loss under my command—the VB-15 gunners were pretty pissed off. We were supposed to be on stand-down and rotated out. After they saw the wounded and counted the dead from their group, they refused to fly. I managed this by simply telling their squadron leader [Mini] that they would be taken off flight status, lose their flight pay, and maybe even face court-martial. I was still going to fly. I guess he relayed the message, because they decided to continue with the missions.

November 13 was a great day for the bomber boys. They sank about eight Jap troopships, but they still kept sending their planes to attack our ships. The airfields were paid another visit, too. The rest of the groups did good work, too, but again we had hard losses in planes and some aircrew. I knew the next day we would repeat the same mission. I led the strike force off the deck before sunrise to look for anything worth bombing. Soon we were engaged by Jap fighters, and I managed to flame an Oscar. Other than that, even the second strike force really found nothing to hit. We had pretty much cleaned their clock, so to speak. That ended my Air Group 15 as a fighting unit, and we boarded the *Bunker Hill* for Pearl. We were going home, and I knew the men had earned it.

After a relaxing leave and weeklong trip, we landed in Washington [State at Puget Sound, Bremerton Naval Shipyard]. During our tour we had lost about seventy-seven aircraft and crews. Many were wounded, and some were never found. But we had shot down over three hundred enemy planes in air combat [318] and even more on the ground [348] and had done a lot of damage to the Jap Navy. We had participated in twenty-three campaigns or so. Later we learned that a few of our pilots and crews had been captured by the Japs and executed. That still pisses me off to no damned end.

These actions by the bombers as well as our fighter squadron created the nickname "Fabled Fifteen" due to our great success record. I was proud as hell of them. The bomber boys were later credited with sinking the Jap super battleship *Musashi*, the sister ship to the *Yamato*. They were something like seventy-thousand-ton monsters, the biggest battleships ever built. They also sank three carriers and a heavy cruiser, and damaged and sank a lot of other ships like destroyers and such and a shitload of transport and troopships.

I went to Washington, DC, on [January 10, 1945] to meet with President Roosevelt so he could award me the Medal of Honor. The usual meets and greets went along with all of that. It was really a national tour, just doing radio shows and talking to people. In March I was given the position of chief of staff to the air fleet commander [commander air fleet] at the Naval Air Station in Norfolk, where I spent almost two years, including the job as commander of carrier air groups. By then, the war was winding down, and I also did some work with the Army, ferrying aircraft loads. Basically, I was shuffled around like a deck of cards. The next trip was a stint at the Armed Forces Staff College in 1947, since I was already in Norfolk. On finishing that, I was made a staff instructor.

I liked being able to see my mom and dad more often, and it really pleased them to no end. I took my dad to see where his father had been a prisoner of war back in the Civil War. It was very cold and icy, and as we were driving back, I hit ice, slid off the road, and rolled the car. Dad was injured, but not badly. He was examined at the hospital [Annapolis] and determined to be OK, so I returned to Norfolk and planned on picking him up later. Not long afterward, I had a call that he was not doing well and was told I needed to get there. His health had not been great due to diabetes, and he went into a coma and died [on February 22, 1947]. That was tough.

I did a year in Norfolk, and then, in 1948, I got a dream assignment in Buenos Aires, Argentina, as the senior naval aviation advisor working with the Argentine Navy, where I was also an instructor at their naval war college. Argentina was in the process of building up its military. This included their army, but especially concerned their air force and navy, and naval aviation in particular, with a focus on creating naval air assets and developing tactics. I had the whole family there. After staying in a hotel for a while, we were able to rent a house. I had a car and an aircraft, a nice Twin Beechcraft with a pilot and all the trimmings. I guess I sort of got to know how MacArthur felt running his empire. I was able to travel all over South America. I loved fishing and this was really paradise.

I completed my tour, and in February of 1951, when Korea was underway, I was assigned as the executive officer aboard the *Franklin D. Roosevelt*. The ship was in the Med [Mediterranean Sea], so I flew there. After an unexpected stopover in Spain, I finally joined the ship and reported to skipper Captain Bill [William V.] Davis [Jr.], replacing one of my old friends, John [L.] Crittenden. As XO, I found myself inundated with paperwork that Davis did not want to deal with, but that was fine. That summer Davis was replaced by Captain Fitzhugh Lee, who had been one of my flight instructors. I stayed there until March 1952 [relieved by Commander Edward C. Outlaw] and then I became planning officer on the staff for ComAirLant [Commander, Airforce, Atlantic], where I was promoted to captain.

I was next assigned as commander of the Naval Air Technical Training Center at Jacksonville [Florida] and sent a year later to be the flight test coordinator at the Naval Air Test Center in Pax [Patuxent] River, Maryland. This was where I trained on jets and learned to fly the Panther [F9F-6] and met a lot of the guys who would later be part of the NASA program. I was then assigned as the operations officer for the Sixth Fleet, which was pretty good duty. I was able to visit a dozen or so countries, and I liked seeing new places. We did a lot of NATO exercises, as you may expect.

In the years that followed, I had the best jobs of all, but commanding the [USS] *Severn* was not one of them. This was an oiler, or a service vessel, and I was less than impressed with the ship and the way it was operated. It was plagued with problems.

I could not wait to get off that ship. I was later to take command of the carrier [USS] *Bonhomme Richard*, but I first had to go [to Kansas] to qualify in the F9F. I had already flown it, so the qualification was quite simple. I was really excited. You cannot have a better job than commanding a carrier, except for flying, I guess. I joined the ship in Manila in February of 1959. Then, as luck would have it, I had a refueling scenario in rough seas. The ship bumped against the tanker, and I had to fight against a formal reprimand. I won, because the tanker captain was not going at the assigned speed and direction, and he was off course.

The bullshit just kept on coming. When we pulled into Japan, a civilian tanker did not adjust his course and we had a slight collision. The bastard filed a claim against the Navy, but we dealt with that shit, and the fault was his. We did, however, have a nice WESTPAC [Western Pacific] cruise where we hit several ports, including Hong Kong. We hit port [San Diego] and brought new aircraft on board such as the [F8U] Crusader and [A4] Skyhawks. It was a new age in naval aviation, to be sure. We were heading out for Hawaii when the curse struck again. We lost a plane and mechanic who was flipped off the deck in high wind. We never recovered him, and that was a bad start.

Then on December 7 [1959], we had a memorial service for the USS *Arizona* Memorial at Pearl Harbor. Dignitaries including Fleet Admiral [Grover B. H. Hall], the CincPac [Commander in Chief Pacific, Admiral Harry D. Felt], congressmen, and all types of flag officers from every branch of the military attended, including my old schoolmate Barry Goldwater, who was a senator representing Arizona. I had come down to meet the admiral when he landed on the flight deck, when my XO told me that we were underway, which was news to me. Sure as hell, we were, and I was there to handle that. We stopped the engines but bashed a few pilings—not a great way to start your day. Well, we did another cruise, and I ended my command tour in February 1960 and took some well-earned leave.

That came to a halt when I was assigned to the Joint Chiefs of Staff in Washington, DC, in 1960. This was a Pentagon assignment, a place where dreams go to die, especially for pilots. If you have read Dante's *Inferno*, you will know what I mean when I say I was in the ninth circle of that purgatory—which is treachery, by the way. This is where you could really see who the career backstabbers were, as opposed to those of us who just wanted to serve and were stuck there for a while. I'll just say that I really did not like it very much. Well, in the planning business, we had to work out what to do with Cuba and Vietnam and the rest is history, I guess.

After that business was over, I had my choice of assignments. In 1962, I went to the North American Air Defense Command in Colorado Springs, near the Air Force Academy, to become the Assistant Deputy Chief of Staff for Operations [to the Commander in Chief for Continental Air Defense Command]. My job was basically to work with the Army and Air Force in establishing protocols for the deployment of any- and everything that was part of the national defense system. This was called the DEW Line, for Defense [or Distant] Early Warning. Radars and all electronic detection systems were basically in a ring around North America tied into Missile Defense and Strategic Air Commands. This was for the detection of incoming missiles, bombers, you name it. Remember, this was the height of the Cold War, and we took this shit pretty seriously. It was a great job, with regular hours and free time.

I was passed over for promotion twice. This pretty much meant I was in terminal pay grade, so I checked out and retired in 1964. I was pretty sure that these were petty political decisions, but it was what it was. I had a friendly admiral once tell me, "Dave, when you walk into a room, many of those guys who outrank you see that little blue-and-white ribbon, Navy Cross,

Silver and Bronze Stars, and it reminds them of how mediocre they are. And those are the pricks who sit on promotion boards." He was right and I knew it, but I know that some of my assignments and personal choices also hindered advancement.

Retirement was not too bad. I sold real estate and caught up on a lot of golf. I always loved fishing, but I had not done much hunting in the last few years. I still get together with old friends from the Navy every now and then and those are good times. But every year or so, there are fewer of us. Time rages on and catches up to us all. All combat fighter pilots are fugitives from the law of averages, but the law always wins in the end.

MEDAL OF HONOR CITATION

Capt. David McCampbell, USN

For conspicuous gallantry and intrepidity at the risk of his life above and beyond the call of duty as commander, Air Group 15, during combat against enemy Japanese aerial forces in the first and second battles of the Philippine Sea. An inspiring leader, fighting boldly in the face of terrific odds, Comdr. McCampbell led his fighter planes against a force of 80 Japanese carrier-based aircraft bearing down on our fleet on 19 June 1944. Striking fiercely in valiant defense of our surface force, he personally destroyed seven hostile planes during this single engagement in which the outnumbering attack force was utterly routed and virtually annihilated. During a major fleet engagement with the enemy on 24 October, Comdr. McCampbell, assisted by but one plane, intercepted and daringly attacked a formation of 60 hostile land-based craft approaching our forces. Fighting desperately but with superb skill against such overwhelming airpower, he shot down nine Japanese planes and, completely disorganizing the enemy group, forced the remainder to abandon the attack before a single aircraft could reach the fleet. His great personal valor and indomitable spirit of aggression under extremely perilous combat conditions reflect the highest credit upon Comdr. McCampbell and the U.S. Naval Service.

Franklin D. Roosevelt, January 10, 1945